A BIRDER'S GUIDE
TO
COASTAL WASHINGTON

by

Bob Morse

Bob Morse

Published by the R. W. Morse Company, Olympia, WA
Copyright © 2001 by the R. W. Morse Company
All rights reserved. No part of this publication may be reproduced, stored in an information or retrieval system, or transmitted, in any form or means, electronic or mechanical, without the express prior written permission of the publisher.
Library of Congress Control Number: 2001118083
ISBN No. 0-9640810-0-8 $18.95 Softcover
First Edition 2001
Second Printing 2002
Third Printing 2002
Printed by
  Mantec Production Company, Hong Kong
Editors
  Bill Tweit and Steve Mlodinow
 Cover and Interior Design
  printcity.com
Maps
  Shawn K. Morse
Cover Photograph
  Fred A. Sharpe

DEDICATION

This book is dedicated to my wife, Maureen, who has endured four decades of being married to a hopelessly hooked bird watcher.

Maureen's untiring encouragement, sage advice, and her balanced perspective, combined with the support of other family members, have helped make this guide a reality.

CONTENTS

Appendices

Please see our website at
www.birdingcoastalwa.com.
Updates and corrections to
this book are posted on the
website.

ACKNOWLEDGMENTS

I would like to thank the many people who have put in a good deal of hard work, time, and energy to create and publish this birding guide. This guide would not have been possible without their contribution.

Scott Horton and Alan Richards spent countless hours in the field observing birds, at home compiling their field observations, and writing information about the birding spots along the coast and are to be commended for their commitment to this project. Scott's focus was the North Coast while Alan's focus was the South Coast. Other birders who have written portions of the text include: Michael Carmody, Rose DuBois, Bruce Fischer, Henry Gilmore, Jim Miller, Bob Norton, Tom Schooley, Terry Sisson, Patrick Sullivan, and Terry Wahl.

Among the many who have reviewed and added immeasurably to the text were Janet Anthony, Una Boyle, Keith Brady, Sally Butts, Eric Cummins, Henry Gilmore, Larry Goldstein, Mike Gurling, Hal Opperman, Mike Patterson, Ted Peterson, Diane Schostak, Fred Sharpe, Greg Shirato, Pat Sisson, Barbara Smith, Bob Steelquist, Patrick Sullivan, Bob Sundstrom, Dan Varland, Richard Youel, and Max Zahn.

I would like to acknowledge the very capable technical review and editorial comments by Bill Tweit and Steve Mlodinow, the Oregon/Washington Regional Editors of *North American Birds*.

Ruth Sullivan has been most generous in donating the use of her marvelous collections of bird photographs. Other photos have been provided by beachdog.com, Keith Brady, George E. Brooks, Brian Caven, James R. Gallagher/Sea and Sage Audubon, Stuart MacKay, Ned Harris, Robert Howson, Peter Knapp, Olympic Coast National Marine Sanctuary, Wayne O'Neil, Art Pavey, Dennis Paulson, Jim Pruske, Terry Sisson, Jeff Skriletz Patrick Sullivan , U. S. Fish and Wildlife Service, and Terry Wahl. Special thanks to Fred Sharpe for the cover photo of a Tufted Puffin and to Greg Marsh of the Olympic National Park for the opportunity to select photographs from their collection. The author's photograph was by Cascade Photographics, Inc. All photographs are copyright protected.

Shawn Morse, who first started building maps for my birding guides in 1985, has created the maps for this guide. Thank you, Shawn, for your countless hours and tireless work.

The coastal Washington checklist was created by Glen and Wanda Hoge, Gene Hunn, Phil Mattocks, Bob Morse, Steve Mlodinow, Russell Rogers, Fred Sharpe, and Bill Tweit.

Dennis Paulson and Terry Wahl have granted permission for use of the habitat classifications as defined and used in *A Guide to Bird Finding in Washington.*

Permission to print accommodation information has been provided by the Forks, Long Beach, Ocean Shores, and Westport/Grayland Chambers of Commerce. Permission to reprint the Ocean Shores map was provided by John L. Scott Real Estate, Ocean Shores under the copyright of North Beach Printing Company, Inc. and John L. Scott Real Estate, Ocean Shores.

To all of the above birders and others who have shared their expertise and knowledge to make this guide more complete and useful, I express my heartfelt thanks.

In such an undertaking as this guide, there are likely to be changes that need to be made. I openly solicit suggestions that will make the guide more accurate and complete. Please send your comments to Bob Morse at rwmorse@attbi.com. Please see our website at **www.birdingcoastalwa.com** for updates and corrections to this book.

INTRODUCTION TO COASTAL WASHINGTON

The coast of Washington is truly an exceptional place. The North Coast is dominated by the Olympic National Park where a stunning and diverse world exists – a fog-shrouded coast with sandy and rocky beaches, spectacular glacier capped mountains, lush meadows, crystal clear lakes, North America's finest temperate rain forest, and one of the most pristine ecosystems in the lower 48 states. Here lies an unspoiled coast with its tidal pools and offshore sea stacks teeming with marine life. Hills of thick conifers envelop the coastal communities. World-class specimens of evergreens grow to gigantic proportions nourished by plentiful coastal rains. Native Americans, whose time here predates Columbus, inhabit these coastal lands. An offshore marine sanctuary, twice the size of Yosemite National Park, protects the pristine coast and its fragile offshore waters and islands.

The South Coast is altogether different. Low rolling hills overlook wide expansive beaches and unspoiled tidal estuaries. Here lies a scenic land of ocean, bays, rivers, and streams with nearby lush forests. Offshore waters teem with tuna, salmon, and bottom fish. The 100 year old oyster industry still flourishes in the pristine waters of Willapa Bay. Step back into yesterday and marvel at the 140-year residences of historic Oysterville or visit Ocean Shores,

1

Washington's most popular coastal resort destination, with its myriad of recreational opportunities. In Long Beach, walk the longest beach in the world. Dine at nationally acclaimed restaurants featuring indigenous seafood or relax at cozy bed and breakfast inns. These are all part of the charm and allure of the South Coast.

More than anything, the coast of Washington is an area of exceptional beauty and scenic splendor.

The 157 miles of the coast of Washington State stretches from the Strait of Juan de Fuca, on the north, to the Columbia River and the State of Oregon, on the south. The coast, including over 800 offshore islands and rocky outcroppings, in addition to its natural beauty, offers a variety of different habitats and exciting birding opportunities.

The area covered in *A Birder's Guide to Coastal Washington* is the entire outer coast of the State of Washington, from Cape Flattery to the Columbia River and up to 30 miles inland from the coastline. The 30 mile limit was set to include such marvelous birding locations as Puget Island, the Julia Butler Hansen Refuge for Columbian White-tailed Deer, Vance Creek, Brady Loop, and up to the timberline in the Olympic Mountains.

High, rocky bluffs and offshore islands dominate the North Coast from Cape Flattery to Point Grenville and are home to over a dozen species of nesting seabirds. At Tatoosh Island, and other offshore islands, storm-petrels, auklets, and puffins nest in burrows dug into grassy hillsides, while Pelagic Cormorant and Common Murre nest on the open cliff ledges. North America's finest temperate rain forest stretches from the water's edge to the mountains of the Olympic National Park, and is home to nesting Blue Grouse, Marbled Murrelet, Spotted Owl, and Varied Thrush. Wet coniferous forests of Douglas fir, western hemlock, western red cedar, and Sitka spruce are found in the Hoh Rain Forest, where trees with hanging moss and the richly carpeted forest floor form a lush landscape. Rainfall here, averaging over 145 inches per year, nourishes the complex and interdependent forest ecosystem.

A significant portion of the North Coast is in Flattery Rocks National Wildlife Refuge (NWR), Quillayute Needles NWR, Copalis Beach NWR, and the Olympic Coast National Marine

Sanctuary. Much of this coast is undeveloped because it is part of the Makah, Ozette, Quileute, Hoh, and Quinault Indian Reservations or within the Olympic National Park.

The Olympic National Park dominates the interior of the northern Olympic peninsula with its rugged snow capped peaks topped by 7,965-foot Mt. Olympus. It is designated as an International Biosphere Reserve and World Heritage Site in recognition of its immense natural value. Two of the more popular park accesses are via Hurricane Ridge near Port Angeles and, at a lower elevation on the west side, via the Hoh River Valley. US Highway 101 is the main north/south corridor through the western part of the Olympic peninsula. In most places, it seems carved out of the dense coniferous forests. This is a region where a significant amount of timber harvesting has occurred, as evidenced by hillsides of clear cuts, yet occasional remote stands of old growth forest still host Spotted Owl.

The South Coast of Washington State (from Moclips to the Columbia River) features wide sandy beaches, grasslands, extensive mudflats and open farmlands. The community of Ocean Shores, with its rich diversity of habitat, has recorded over 290 species of birds. Jetties host Wandering Tattler, Surfbird, and Rock Sandpiper while nearby beaches and *Salicornia* marshes hold Pacific Golden-Plover, and the rare Sharp-tailed Sandpiper. Ocean Shores seems to be a magnet for rare birds in Washington, including Mottled Petrel, Manx Shearwater, Eurasian Dotterel, Bristle-thighed Curlew, Bar-tailed Godwit, Curlew Sandpiper, Ivory Gull, Least Tern, Long-billed Murrelet, Horned Puffin, Yellow Wagtail, and McKay's Bunting.

One of the true treasures of the Washington coast is the Grays Harbor National Wildlife Refuge in Hoquiam. The refuge's 1500 acres of mudflats provide a critical food source and staging area for hundreds of thousands of shorebirds that stop on their migration from South America to the arctic each spring. Pelagic trips out of Westport offer the birder the opportunity to see albatrosses, shearwaters, petrels, jaegers, and auklets, among other pelagic specialties.

Tokeland, further south along the coast, provides a reliable spot to study long-legged shorebirds such as Willet, Whimbrel, Long-billed Curlew, the rare Bar-tailed Godwit, and Marbled Godwit. The 13,900 acre Willapa National Wildlife Refuge hosts a wide assortment of wintering waterfowl with impressive numbers of Canada Goose (including several different subspecies), Brant, and a myriad of ducks.

The Long Beach Peninsula and especially Leadbetter Point are regular migration stops for Red Knot in spring and Pacific Golden-Plover and occasional Sharp-tailed Sandpiper in fall. Snowy Plovers nest at the tip of Leadbetter Point. Fort Canby State Park, at the mouth of the Columbia River, with its sandy shore, rock jetty, coniferous and broadleaf woods, freshwater lakes and marshes, and rocky cliffs, provides an impressive assortment of resident and migrant birds.

Aberdeen (population 17,000), the largest coastal city, is located midway along the coast on the shore of Grays Harbor. Aberdeen, less than three hours from Seattle and Portland, has a rich history of logging and timber based industries. Today, with more focus on the environment, the town is diversifying into service and tourism activities. As the only deep-water port on the coast north of San Francisco, cruise ships and exporting are becoming a larger part of their economy.

The other larger towns of the coast are Ocean Shores, a retirement community; Westport, a ship building and fishing community; and Ilwaco, a fishing-based community. North of Aberdeen, the largest town is Forks which still has a timber-based economy. Many of the smaller coastal towns such as Moclips, Pacific Beach, and those on the Long Beach Peninsula, attract large numbers of tourists during the summer months.

A birder in Washington State could see up to 365 species of birds by visiting the Washington Coast. This represents 80% of the species that have been found in the state. With this many species, it is easy to see why the Washington coast is such an attraction for birders. Many come to see the specialty birds and hope for the rarity that occasionally appears. Special attention has been placed in this guide on the Coastal Specialties and where to look for them.

How to Use This Guide

GENERAL

The purpose of *A Birder's Guide to Coastal Washington* is to give birders a useful tool in their quest to find birds along the coast of Washington. The Introduction to Coastal Washington gives a general overview of coastal Washington and why it is such an amazing place to watch birds. Geography and Climate describes the geography and climate of the coast. The coastal habitats are described in next chapter.

A map, showing the entire coast and many of the prime birding locations, is provided inside the back cover. Map symbols are also shown inside the back cover.

Over 160 of the better coastal birding spots along the coast have been described in Coastal Birding Areas with a map, a discussion of the birds found at each location, and in some cases a photograph of the site. Each of these birding locales is highlighted with bold lettering. All areas described in the book are public property and available for use by birders.

A checklist of the coastal birds and their seasonal distribution, in the appendix, provides birders information on when the different species may be found as well as a way to keep a record of their sightings. It also provides a means to determine when to visit the coast.

Coastal Specialties, identifies the 82 target birds that most birders seek when they come to the coast and discusses where and when they may be found. Special effort has been made to identify the location of these birds in the text. Coastal Specialties also provides color photographs of most of the coastal specialty birds.

A list of coastal birding organizations, their phone numbers, and web addresses has been added as an appendix. Useful birding web site addresses have also been added. To learn more about Forest Passes, parking decals, weather, tides, and maps and to assist in finding accommodations, a list of the Chambers of Commerce, national and state camping locations, and detailed accommodation information by location has been included in More Coastal Information.

Although photographs of many of the specialty birds have been included in this guide, the guide is not intended to serve as a bird identification guide. There are a number of good identification guides such as the National Geographic *Field Guide to the Birds of North America*, Peterson Field Guides, *Western Birds*, Kaufman Focus Guides *Birds of North America*, and National Audubon Society *The Sibley Guide to Birds*. The focus of **A Birder's Guide to Coastal Washington** is on where to find the birds, not on species identification, although selected identification information has been provided in the section on Coastal Specialties.

MILEAGES

Many of the highways along the coast have milepost (MP) markers along the highway denoting the mileage. The mileposts are in one-mile increments. To assist in noting a specific location along the road, mileages have been noted in tenths of a mile in the text. For example, "turn right at MP 16.5 onto Curry Road" will require that the birder note the mileage at MP 16 and measure off an additional 0.5 miles to get the proper distance to the Curry Road turn.

Sometimes, the roads do not have MP markers. In these cases, the text will state "turn left at 10.3 miles from the main highway" indicating that the birder needs to take a mileage reading at the main highway.

A note on travel time is appropriate. The large coastal map and each of the site maps have scales that show distances. Because many of the major roads along the coast are twisting, well traveled in summer, or may have heavily laden logging trucks, the travel time between the places along the coast may be deceptive. Here are some guidelines that may be useful (add time spent birding):

Between	Miles	Approximate Travel Time
Seattle and Aberdeen	109	2 hours, 15 min
Aberdeen and Westport	22	30 min
Aberdeen and Ocean Shores	22	35 min
Aberdeen and Lake Quinault	44	1 hour, 10 min
Aberdeen and Forks	98	2 hours, 15 min
Aberdeen and Taholah	39	1 hour
Aberdeen and Tokeland	32	50 min
Aberdeen and Ilwaco	71	1 hour, 30 min
Aberdeen and Port Angeles	160	4 hours
Aberdeen and Portland, OR	142	2 hours, 45 min
Aberdeen and Raymond	25	35 min
Forks and Lake Quinault	68	1 hour, 20 min
Forks and Port Angeles	58	1 hour, 30 min
Forks and Neah Bay	49	1 hour, 30 min
Forks and La Push	16	25 min
Raymond and Ilwaco	50	1 hour, 10 min
Ilwaco and Cathlamet	51	1 hour, 10 min
Cathlamet and I-5 (Kelso)	27	40 min

REPORTING RARE BIRDS

If you are fortunate enough to discover an unusual or rare bird in your visit to the coast, please take a few minutes and help your fellow birders by reporting what you saw. The sooner you report your sighting, the quicker other birders can enjoy your success.

You can report your sightings either by phone or email.

By Phone.

Call 206-281-9172, the Washington Ornithological Society (WOS) rare bird alert. Follow the prompts. When the prompt asks for the number of Chickadee species seen in Washington State, enter 4. Be sure to leave a phone number where you can reached.

By Email.

Send an email to Bruce Fischer at aberdeen@bigfoot.com with the details of what you saw, when, where (be specific), and how you can be reached. Ask Bruce to enter your sighting into the Tweeters Daily Digest (the state bird chat line). The Tweeters web address is:

http://www.scn.org/earth/tweeters/index.html.

For sightings of birds that have been recorded less than 5 times (as noted on page 4 of the checklist in the appendix) please take a few moments to write a detailed description of the rarity with all the salient field marks and mail it to Phil Mattocks, Secretary, WOS Records Committee, 5421 Hanson Road, Ellensburg, WA 98926.

GEOGRAPHY AND CLIMATE

GEOGRAPHY

High rocky cliffs, offshore islands, and rocky outcroppings dominate the North Coast of Washington. This section of the coast receives abundant amounts of winter rain. The rainy season lasts from October through April and close to 200 inches of rain falls each year on the western slopes of Mt. Olympus, the largest amount in the lower 48 states. This rain, moderate temperatures, and coastal fog nurtures the world-famous temperate rain forest as best exemplified by the Hoh Rain Forest. World-class specimens of Douglas fir, Sitka spruce, western red cedar, and western hemlock exist in the pristine environment of the Olympic National Park.

The forests of the Olympic Peninsula support an active timber industry. Abundant evidence of logging can be seen in the second and third growth forests visible along US 101. During the decade of the 1990s, the timber industry made a sometimes painful transition from harvesting and exporting mostly old growth timber to harvesting and locally processing smaller timber from managed forests.

The rugged coastline from Cape Flattery to Copalis Head and the offshore waters are part of the 3,310 square mile Olympic Coast National Marine Sanctuary. This sanctuary is dedicated to the protection of the wild, pristine coast, its rugged sea stacks, kelp beds, and nutrient rich coastal waters.

The South Coast is home to the Willapa and Grays Harbor National Wildlife Refuges. The Grays Harbor NWR is one of only eight sites in North America to be recognized as a Western Hemisphere Shorebird Reserve Network Site. With their sandy beaches, mudflats, and nutrient rich estuaries, these refuges provide unique and critical habitat to large numbers of migrating shorebirds in spring and wintering waterfowl. State parks including Fort Canby, Leadbetter, Ocean City, Griffiths-Priday, Bottle Beach, and Westhaven cover the South Coast and provide an assortment of different habitats and a wide variety of birds.

CLIMATE

The Pacific Northwest coast enjoys a consistently mild maritime climate. Cool temperatures prevail in both summer and winter with prolonged periods of rain in winter.

Much of the coastal climate is influenced by the weather patterns of the Pacific Ocean. In the summer, high-pressure cells tend to dominate the north Pacific bringing sunny stable weather to the Washington coast. Generally, summers are fair with afternoon temperatures averaging between 65 and 70 degrees. Winds at this time of year normally are from the west and northwest.

In winter, high-pressure cells are replaced by low-pressure systems bringing prolonged periods of moisture from the tropical Pacific or from the Gulf of Alaska driven by west or southwest winds. Average afternoon temperatures are in the 40s and 50s. Severe winter storms occasionally strike the coast with strong winds, driving rains, and can be accompanied by high tides.

Rainfall in the region varies by location. The temperate rain forest of the Olympic Peninsula has the wettest winter climate of the lower 48 states with annual precipitation exceeding

140" while 30 miles west on the coast, Kalaloch receives an average of 90" of rainfall. The Willapa Hills, in southwest Washington, average 100" per year. Coastal communities such as Aberdeen and Westport only average 80" to 90" per year.

It seldom snows along the coast due to the mild ocean temperatures but Mt. Olympus and other Olympic Mountains above 5,500 feet in elevation are snow covered year round and areas over 3,000 feet normally have snow on the ground all winter.

Fog forms along the coast during the months of July, August, and early September when warmer temperatures occur along the coast. At this time of year, fog banks and low clouds form over the ocean and move inland at night. The tops of the clouds are normally below 3000 feet so the higher elevations may be clear while the valleys are shrouded in fog. Morning clouds or fog may occur at other times of the year along the coast when the weather is clear, but normally burn off as the day progresses.

COASTAL HABITATS

O ne of the reasons there are so many species of birds along the Washington coast is the great variety of habitat found in this part of the state. Since a bird's selection of habitat is linked to its food and nesting preferences, the more habitats there are in an area, the larger the number of species of birds. The habitats as defined by Wahl and Paulson in *A Guide to Bird Finding in Washington* have been used in this book. Along the coast, these habitats include: open salt water, rocky shores, sandy shores, mudflats, salt marshes, freshwater lakes and marshes, wet coniferous forests, broadleaf forests, shrubby thickets, parks, gardens, and farmlands.

Open Salt Water

Keith Brady

13

The open salt water with its rich supply of marine life provides food for loons, albatrosses, petrels, waterfowl, and alcids. This includes all the offshore waters of the coast, the Strait of Juan de Fuca, as well as the large bays such as Grays Harbor and Willapa. Most of the pelagic salt water species are best seen during a pelagic boat trip. These have been marked with a "P" in the checklist in the appendix. For birders wishing to remain on land, the best chance to see pelagic species is from a rock jetty or promontory after a storm.

Rocky Shores

Keith Brady

Rocky shores include the offshore islands that are home to over a dozen species of nesting seabirds. It also includes the high rocky cliffs, rocky beaches, and rocky outcroppings that dominate the North Coast. There are a few rocky shores on the South Coast such as the rock jetties at Ocean Shores, Westport, Fort Canby, and the rock breakwaters at Tokeland and along the Columbia River.

Sandy Shores, Mudflats, Salt Marshes

Keith Brady

The South Coast has a predominance of sandy shores, mudflats, and salt marshes. This is home to the hundreds of thousands of shorebirds and waterfowl, which migrate along the coast and those which nest here. This region also includes open areas and dune grasses surrounding the shorelines and salt marshes. Good examples of this habitat include the Ocean Shores Game Range, Grays Harbor NWR, Bottle Beach State Park, Willapa NWR, and much of the Long Beach Peninsula.

Freshwater Lakes, Rivers, and Marshes

George E. Brooks

Freshwater lakes, rivers, and marshes are common along the North and South Coasts and provide nesting and foraging opportunities for grebes, waterfowl, rails, and shorebirds. Examples of this habitat include Lake Quinault, Ocean Shores lakes and canals, Friends Landing, and Vance Creek Park.

Wet Coniferous Forests

Keith Brady

Wet coniferous forests are the dominant habitat of coastal Washington with their Douglas fir, western red cedar, western hemlock, and Sitka spruce. Patches of old growth still exist, but most of these forests have been replaced by second or third growth trees. In the higher elevations, Pacific silver fir, Alaska cedar, mountain hemlock, and subalpine fir occur. Some of the better examples of wet coniferous forest include Willoughby Ridge, the hills around Lake Quinault, the Quinault Ridge Road, and upper Wynoochee Valley.

Broadleaf Forests

Bob Morse

In the wetter parts of the coast, broadleaf forests of deciduous trees are common. Red alder is the predominant species accompanied by bigleaf maple, vine maple, and black cottonwood. In many areas, the broadleaf forests grow among the coniferous forests. Examples of broadleaf forests include the road to Cape Flattery, the Hoko Ozette Road, the Hoh Rain Forest, and along Lake Quinault's South Shore Road.

Shrubby Thickets

Bob Morse

Shrubby thickets are common undergrowth in the coastal areas with their tangles of blackberry, huckleberry, salmonberry, elderberry, salal, and ferns. This habitat exists along many of the roadsides adjoining wet coniferous and broadleaf forests.

Parks and Gardens

Bob Morse

Typical urban habitats such as parks and gardens exist in and surrounding the towns of the coast.

Farmlands

Bob Morse

The South Coast has a fair amount of pasturelands, open fields, and farmlands, some for dairy animals, and others for agricultural and recreational uses. Puget Island, south of Cathlamet, is a good example of open fields with borders of brushy thickets, and occasional ponds and sloughs. Other examples are the Ocean Shores Golf Course, Damon Point, Monte Brady Loop Road, Wenzel Slough Road in Elma, the lower end of the Wynoochee Valley Road, the fields along the Palix River, and Chinook Valley Road.

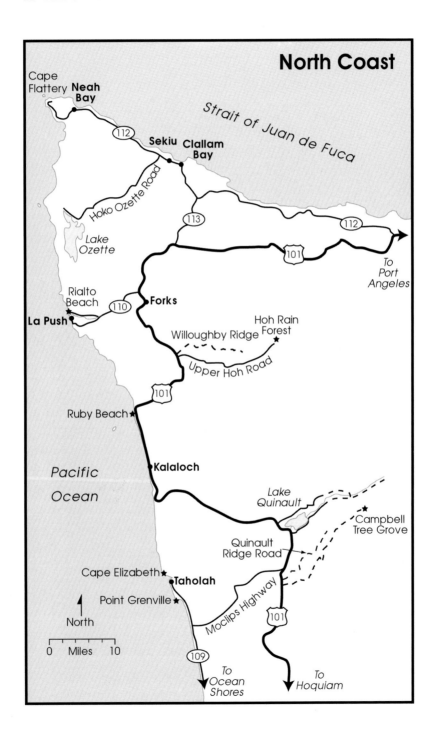

North Coast

Cape
Flattery **Neah
Bay**

Strait of Juan de Fuca

112

**Sekiu Clallam
Bay**

Hoko Ozette Road

113

101

112

*Lake
Ozette*

*To
Port
Angeles*

Rialto
Beach 110 **Forks**

La Push

Hoh Rain
Willoughby Ridge Forest

Upper Hoh Road

101

Ruby Beach

*Pacific

Ocean*

Kalaloch

*Lake
Quinault*

Campbell
Tree Grove

Quinault
Ridge Road

Cape Elizabeth **Taholah**

Point Grenville

Moclips Highway

101

North

0   Miles   10

109

*To
Ocean
Shores*

*To
Hoquiam*

Coastal Birding Areas

NORTH COAST

The North Coast of Washington State starts at Cape Flattery, the most northwestern part of the lower 48 United States. But, since birders have to travel through the Strait of Juan de Fuca fishing villages of Clallam Bay, Sekiu, and Neah Bay to reach Cape Flattery, the better birding spots along the way have been included in this guide.

Our description of the North Coast starts along the Strait of Juan De Fuca in the town of Clallam Bay. To get to Clallam Bay, go west from Port Angeles on State Route (SR) 112 or north from Forks on US 101, SR 113, and SR 112.

Clallam Bay/Sekiu

Clallam Bay Park (day use only) is straight ahead, just as the highway bends left in the town of Clallam Bay. This park offers access to the beach and river mouth and has good potential for Red-throated, Pacific, and Common Loons, Horned, Red-necked, and Western Grebes, Pelagic Cormorant, Harlequin Duck, all three scoters, Red-breasted Merganser, Common Murre, Pigeon Guillemot, Marbled and Ancient (winter) Murrelets, Rhinoceros Auklet, and an assortment of gulls at the river mouth. The footbridge crosses a small river where Green Heron and Lesser Yellowlegs have appeared. Check the alder trees and the shrubby thickets along the riverbank for passerines during migration. Beyond the Slip Point Lighthouse, to the east, are beaches where glass balls have occasionally washed ashore and marine fossils have been found.

At the west end of town, the **lagoon** behind the beach can

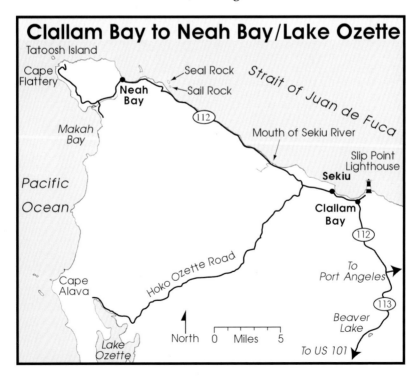

Clallam Bay to Neah Bay/Lake Ozette

Tatoosh Island
Cape Flattery
Seal Rock
Sail Rock
Strait of Juan de Fuca
Neah Bay
112
Makah Bay
Mouth of Sekiu River
Slip Point Lighthouse
Sekiu
Pacific Ocean
Clallam Bay
112
Hoko Ozette Road
To Port Angeles
Cape Alava
113
Beaver Lake
North   0   Miles   5
Lake Ozette
To US 101

occasionally hold a surprising variety of wintering waterfowl. Check for Greater White-fronted Goose, Trumpter Swan, Common Goldeneye, and Hooded and Red-breasted Mergansers. Pullouts here are limited but look for a wide shoulder out of the way of traffic.

Less than a quarter-mile further west, stop at the Spring Tavern parking lot with its elevated view of **Clallam Bay** and scope the open bay and near shore kelp beds.

A pullout at MP 15.6, across from the Breakwater Resort and coffee shop, offers another view of the bay and its birds.

Check the protected waters of the jetty and marina in **Sekiu** (pronounced "Sea-cue") for grebes, cormorants, scoters, and gulls. In winter, check offshore for Ancient Murrelet. King and Silver Salmon are caught in the waters along the strait from Clallam Bay to Neah Bay and sport fishing is an important part of the local economy.

Neah Bay

Proceed west on winding SR 112 toward Neah Bay. In winter, the offshore waters hold large numbers of loons, grebes, diving ducks, and alcids, but parking along this stretch of the highway is limited and logging trucks travel by at amazing speeds. Use the pullouts and park well off the road. Gray Whales summer along this portion of the strait and Sea Otters sometimes appear in the nearshore kelp beds. The nearshore waters between Clallam Bay and Neah Bay are some of the best places to find Marbled Murrelet, especially in the morning. Rocky outcroppings along the shore may host Black Oystercatcher.

At the **mouth of the Sekiu River**, pull off to the right at MP 9.5 and walk back to the bridge to view the flocks of bathing and roosting gulls, which in winter may include Herring, Thayer's, and Glaucous (rare). The best viewpoint for **Seal and Sail Rocks** (about ¼ - ½ mile off shore and the only seabird nesting islands along this shoreline) is at MP 0.8 on an outside curve just before

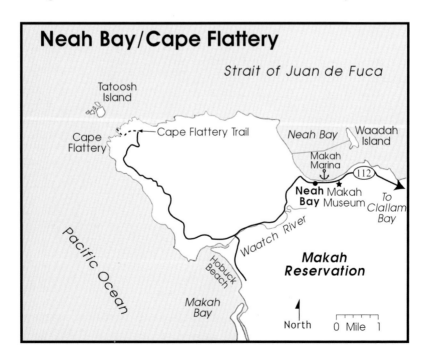

Neah Bay/Cape Flattery

Strait of Juan de Fuca

Tatoosh Island

Cape Flattery

Cape Flattery Trail

Neah Bay

Waadah Island

Makah Marina

112

Neah Makah
Bay Museum

To Clallam Bay

Pacific Ocean

Waatch River

Hobuck Beach

Makah Bay

Makah Reservation

North

0 Mile 1

the sign for the Snow Creek Resort. Scope the surrounding waters for Gray Whale, Sea Otter, Harbor Seal, and a variety of birds including Tufted Puffin (summer) and Marbled Murrelet.

Continue west into the town of **Neah Bay** on the Makah Reservation. The Makahs have occupied this land for at least 2,000 years and are the only indigenous people outside of Alaska to hunt whales, a custom they revived in 1999, amidst considerable controversy. Look for Bald Eagles, which are especially abundant in March and April. Check the waters at the **Makah Marina**, around the Old Fish Dock (take first paved road to right after coming down hill into Neah Bay), other docks, and the bay for loons (including Yellow-billed, winter, rare), grebes, all the diving ducks, gulls (including Thayer's, winter, rare), alcids (Ancient Murrelet, winter), Steller's and California Sea Lions, and Harbor Seal. The base of the jetty protecting the harbor entrance may have Black Oystercatcher, Black Turnstone, and Surfbird. Bad weather sometimes finds pelagic species seeking refuge in the bay. Overhead, good numbers of Turkey Vultures may appear in April and May as they prepare for their northern flight over the Strait of Juan de Fuca.

Puffin Adventures, based in Neah Bay, offers 3 hour bird watching tours to the waters off Cape Flattery and around Tatoosh Island where close observation of Tufted Puffin and other alcids is possible, especially during the breeding season (May through early August). Contact them at 1-888-305-2437 or www.olypen.com/puffinadventures/.

Take time to visit the exceptional Makah Museum to learn about the traditional way of life of the Native American fishermen and whalers ($4.00 entrance fee, closed Monday and Tuesday in winter). Museum exhibits include numerous artifacts from Lake Ozette, boats, a landscape replica, photographs, and original native art. Services in Neah Bay include lodging, restaurants, gas station, Washburn's General Store (a source of Native American art and smoked salmon), and a public restroom (next to Washburn's).

In Neah Bay, follow the road west along the waterfront through town. Past the Makah Senior Center, check the small creek as it enters the bay and nearby beaches for waterfowl and shorebirds (3 Emperor Geese were here in March 1985). The creek mouth is a good spot to study gulls.

The road to Cape Flattery veers left past the Makah Senior Center. Turn right at the second intersection (just past the Indian Health Center building). At the fish hatchery sign, half a block ahead, turn left. The road continues through alder trees and then parallels the open marshes of the Waatch (pronounced "Wy-atch") River. A visit at one of the higher tides will make it feel like you are out on the bay. Turn left at the hatchery sign and cross the **Waatch River**. After the bridge, turn right on a dirt road toward Hobuck Beach and **Makah Bay**.

The long sandy **Hobuck Beach**, on the right, holds shorebirds during migration. There are a number of places to park off the road if you avoid the soft sand. Because of its remote location, it is advisable to lock valuables in the trunk.

The rocky shores, as the Waatch River enters the Makah Bay, should be checked for Wandering Tattler, turnstones, and Surfbird in migration. The offshore surf often has loons, grebes, scoters, and occasional alcids. Harlequin Ducks are common around the offshore rocks. (See below for more information on the river mouth access from the north side of the river)

Being the northwest corner of the lower 48 United States and the first open bay and marsh after crossing the Strait of Juan de Fuca, this should make Makah Bay and the Waatch River valley a natural spot for unusual North American and Asian vagrants. So far, few have been reported, probably because this remote location is so under-birded.

Cape Flattery

When returning from Makah Bay, cross the Waatch River, go left after the bridge and drive past the Tribal Center.

A small dirt track on the left, just as the road starts up the hill (opposite the south end of the old Air Force base) leads to the **mouth of the Waatch River**. This road may be impassable but can be walked to a vantage point, on the north side of the river, which allows studies of shorebirds and gulls roosting at the river mouth and Harlequin Duck around the offshore rocks.

Continue up the hill about 5 miles through mixed broadleaf and coniferous forests and shrubby thickets to the Cape Flattery trailhead. Along the way, expect to hear or see Rufous Hummingbird (among the flowering salmonberry), woodpeckers, Northwestern Crow, Chestnut-backed Chickadee, Brown Creeper, Winter Wren, Golden-crowned Kinglet, Swainson's and Varied Thrushes, Orange-crowned, Black-throated Gray, and Wilson's Warblers, Purple Finch, and Red Crossbill.

Park at the trailhead and take your scope down the ³/₄ mile improved **Cape Flattery Trail** to spectacular overlooks of the Pacific Ocean and the Strait of Juan de Fuca. This is the northwestern tip of the lower 48 states. There are four viewing platforms with picnic tables at the overlook. The seabird watching can vary from fair to excellent, but the scenery is always superb

Among the birds to watch for are Pigeon Guillemot and Tufted Puffin, which nest immediately below the overlook (guillemots in large caves at the base of the 100-foot cliffs). Search for all species of loons and as well as Sooty Shearwater (offshore in summer and fall), Bald Eagle, Peregrine Falcon, Black Oystercatcher, Common Murre, Marbled Murrelet, Rhinoceros Auklet, Black and Vaux's Swifts (summer). With a telescope, Cassin's Auklet occasionally may be seen 1/4 mile north in tide rips. Marine mammals include Gray Whale (April), Steller's Sea Lion,

Harbor Seal, Harbor Porpoise, and Sea Otter.

The status of Black Swift along this part of the North Coast is uncertain. There have been sightings at dawn, dusk, and during overcast days from this area and there is suspicion that they may nest along this part of the coast. To gain a better understanding of the Black Swift status, please report any sightings of Black Swift to the Regional Editors of *North American Birds* (see Coastal Birding Organizations in the Appendices).

Tatoosh Island   Olympic Coast National Marine Sanctuary

Tatoosh Island, ½ mile offshore, supports a variety of breeding seabirds including Fork-tailed and Leach's Storm Petrels (both are pelagic and return to their burrows at night), Pelagic Cormorant, Glaucous-winged Gull, Common Murre, Pigeon Guillemot, Rhinoceros Auklet, and Tufted Puffin. The waters around Tatoosh Island may be the best place in the state to see Tufted Puffin during their nesting season (May through early August). Access to Tatoosh Island is restricted but a spotting scope allows views of the island and its birds. Interestingly, the Tatoosh Island lighthouse was built in 1857 and remains one of the oldest operating lighthouses along the West Coast.

In Sekiu and Neah Bay, adventurous and experienced birders can rent a skiff to explore the nearshore waters, including those around Tatoosh Island. Less adventurous birders can make arrangements with Puffin Adventures to tour the waters around Tatoosh Island. A few lucky birders at Neah Bay have seen Leach's Storm Petrel at dawn as they return to their nests on Tatoosh Island.

Lake Ozette

Lake Ozette   Olympic National Park

Return to SR 112. At MP 12.5, turn right onto the Hoko Ozette Road. Proceed 21 miles to the Lake Ozette Ranger Station in the Olympic National Park. Lake Ozette is the third largest natural body of fresh water in Washington and over 300 feet deep.

The **Hoko Ozette Road** cuts through commercial forests of Douglas fir and western hemlock of varying ages. The road parallels the Hoko River and is bordered by mature stands of mixed conifer and broadleaf species (red alder, bigleaf maple, and black cottonwood). In the summer, birds here include Vaux's Swifts, Olive-sided, Willow, Hammond's, and Pacific-slope Flycathers, Swainson's Thrush (common), Western Tanager, and Black-headed Grosbeak.

At the **Ranger Station and campground** at Lake Ozette, search the lake for Common Loon (may nest here) and Bald Eagle. Varied Thrush and Red Crossbill call from the nearby coniferous forests. In the winter, Trumpeter Swan and a variety of loons, grebes, and ducks may be found on the lake. A male Northern Parula visited here in June 2001.

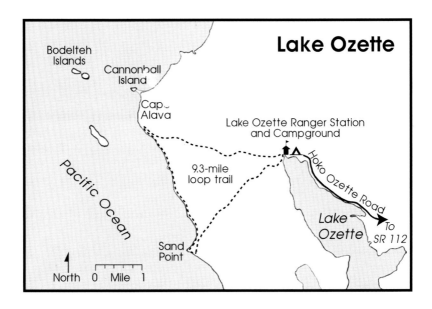

For excellent opportunities to enjoy the birds, marine mammals, and spectacular views of pristine forests and the coastline, hike to **Cape Alava** (3.3 miles) or take the 9.3 mile **Cape Alava-Sand Point-Ranger Station Loop**. This loop hike includes three miles among the tidepools and sea stacks of the coast and is one of the most popular hikes in the Olympic National Park. Check tide tables to be certain that the beach part of this trip is crossed during low tide to avoid being caught by incoming tides. Reservations are required to camp on the beach in summer and may be made by calling 360-565-3100.

Sea Otters can be seen regularly in the kelp beds north and south of Cannonball Island (Cannonball Island is connected to Cape Alava by a narrow spit at low tide but, as a sacred Makah site, is off limits to tourists).

A 480-year-old Makah village was excavated near Cape Alava and its artifacts form the basis of many of the exhibits at the Makah Museum.

Northwest of Cape Alava and one and a half miles

offshore, lie the Bodelteh Islands, home to thousands of nesting Fork-tailed Storm Petrel and Cassin's Auklet. Both species nest here but leave and return from their nests only at night, allowing little opportunity for observation.

Return to SR 112 and continue south along SR 113 through clear-cuts and managed coniferous forests. **Beaver Lake**, just south of MP 4 along SR 113, (see Clallam Bay to Neah Bay/ Lake Ozette map) offers picnic tables and the opportunity to search the lake for grebes and waterfowl. Proceed south to US 101 and Forks.

La Push and Rialto Beach

At MP 193.1 on US 101, turn right at the La Push Mora sign onto SR 110. The road to La Push travels through Douglas fir, western hemlock, and Sitka spruce forests and crosses into the Olympic National Park as it nears the Quileute Indian village of La Push. Inside the national park, the 1.3-mile **Third Beach Trail**, on the left, leads to a wilderness beach with its sweep of sand and sea stacks. It may be possible to hear or see Spotted Owl in the first ½-mile of the trail, and with a flashlight it can be safely walked in the dark. Further along, **Second Beach Trail**, on the left, is a 0.7-mile trail leading through spruce trees (listen for Red Crossbill) to a beach where cormorants, Tufted Puffin, Sea Otter, and Harbor Seal may be seen. At low tide, shallow pools along the shore are teeming with intertidal life. Marbled Murrelet can be seen just off the kelp line at Second and Third Beaches. Check for Japanese glass floats in early

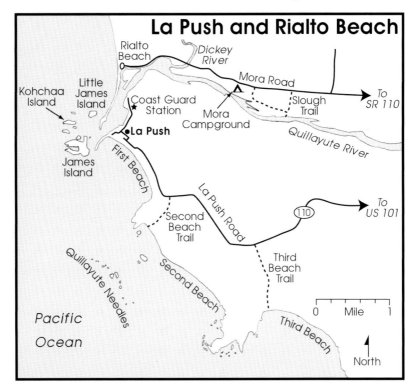

La Push and Rialto Beach

spring along these beaches. Peregrine Falcon nest at Second Beach. The **Quillayute Needles**, ¹/₂-mile offshore, host thousands of nesting seabirds including the state's largest colony of Leach's Storm-Petrel.

On the outskirts of **La Push**, Lonesome Creek RV Park (360-374-4338) provides camping, RV accommodations, and a store. Next door, the rustic La Push Ocean Park Resort (800-487-1267) has a motel and cabins. After the cabins, the road turns right onto Alder Street and then left onto River Street. In a short distance, River St. ends at a "T" intersection. Go left and bear right along a dirt road to an elevated rocky overlook where good views are possible of the Quillayute River and **First Beach** to the south, with the Quillayute Needles in the distance and the open ocean visible beyond. Migrating Gray Whales are in large numbers off First Beach during their spring migration (especially April).

La Push with boat basin
and Quillayute River

Olympic National Park

The largest offshore islands to the west are James Island, far left, and Little James Island, far right. The larger island in the middle is called Kohchaa, which in the Quileute language means "gathering place for sea gull eggs and seafood." Peregrine Falcon nest on **James Island**. Tufted Puffins nest in burrows (May through early August) on **Kohchaa Island** and may be seen with a spotting scope. This may be the only spot in Washington State where you lean against the front bumper of your car and observe Tufted Puffins.

La Push offshore islands Kohchaa (L),   Bob Morse
Little James (R), and Quillayute River

La Push is notable for its easily observed concentration of gulls that roost on the gravel bar in the **Quillayute River** as it enters the ocean. Look for a large concentration of California Gulls in August and September. Also search for Western, Glaucous-winged, and the more common Glaucous-winged X Western hybrid (locally known as "Olympic Gull"). In winter, check for Mew, Herring, Thayer's, Glaucous (rare) Gulls, and Black-legged Kittiwake. In summer and fall, Brown Pelican, Heermann's Gull, and Caspian Tern can be found here.

Harlequin Duck, all three scoters, both goldeneyes, Bufflehead, and Common and Red-breasted Mergansers, are usually in the river channel. Bald Eagle and Peregrine Falcon constantly stir up the gull flocks. The Northwestern Crow (smaller and higher pitched) can be seen here but see the note about this species in the Coastal Specialties Appendix. On the rock jetty, check for Black Oystercatcher, Black Turnstone, and in the spring and fall, Wandering Tattler. Check for loons and grebes in the boat basin (an Emperor Goose spent the winter of 1994-1995 here) and use a scope to check for offshore Marbled Murrelet. Proceed past the boat basin and past the Coast Guard station to the end of the road and check the Quillayute River for additional birds.

Return on SR 110 to the junction of La Push and Mora Roads and go left on Mora Road towards Rialto Beach. Just as Mora Road enters the Olympic National Park, the **Slough Trail** leads off to the left through a native forest of western hemlock and Sitka spruce to the Quillayute River. A small parking area is nearby. Along the trail, look and listen for Varied Thrush, Red Crossbill (in spruce trees), and other birds of the coniferous woods. Bald Eagles have nested where the trail meets the river.

The **Mora Campground** is located just inside the Olympic National Park and is situated in the middle of an old growth forest on the bank of the Quillayute River. Naturalist programs (summer) explain the ecology of a healthy native forest and other elements of the natural and human history of the area.

Continue west on Mora Road. A pullout on the left gives a view of the Dickey and Quillayute rivers as they merge. Bufflehead, Common Goldeneye, and Red-breasted and Common Mergansers are regular here and a variety of other water birds are seen occasionally. This is a good location to watch Native-American fishermen (or more commonly, Harbor Seals) try to catch salmon or steelhead migrating upstream.

The road ends at a parking lot in **Rialto Beach**, the starting point for beach hikers heading for the Hole in the Wall, Lake Ozette, and other points north. To the south, a one-mile rocky and sandy spit parallels the Quillayute River and ends near the rock outcroppings visible from La Push. Check for rock shorebirds, Black Oystercatcher, and scan the roosting gull flocks. A picnic area is near the parking lot at Rialto Beach.

Return to US 101 and turn right. Proceed south through Forks where accommodations and restaurants are available. Along US 101 on the south side of town, sits the Forks Chamber of Commerce and the Forks Timber Museum which features displays of logging, pioneer life, and the history of the coastal Indians (open Monday through Saturday 9:00 a.m. to 4:00 p.m., April through October).

Willoughby Ridge

For great summer birding (May to July), this loop trip gives the opportunity for spectacular views and easy access into the higher elevations of the old growth forests and their birdlife.

A high clearance vehicle is suggested, but four-wheel drive is not needed.

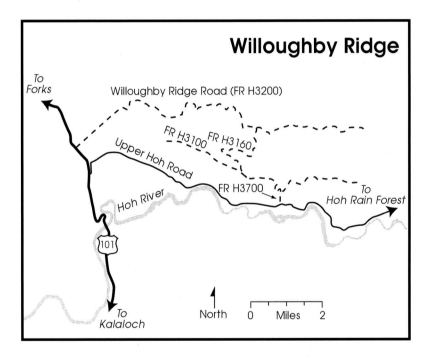

To Forks

Willoughby Ridge Road (FR H3200)

FR H3100   FR H3160

Upper Hoh Road

Hoh River

FR H3700

To Hoh Rain Forest

101

To Kalaloch

North   0   Miles   2

At MP 179.3 on US 101, turn left onto Forest Road H3200 **(Willoughby Ridge Road)**. The sign for H3200 is easy to miss. Make a note of the mileage reading at this point. Continue east through young, commercial forests of western hemlock, western red cedar, and Douglas fir. The first two miles of the road proceeds through relatively flat commercial forest plantations of a variety of ages. Bird the clear cuts, edges, and second growth for Willow and Pacific-slope Flycatchers, Hutton's Vireo, MacGillivray's and Wilson's Warblers, and Spotted Towhee. (A "clear cut" is an area of conifers that has been commercially harvested, leaving open areas with brushy thickets and young conifers).

The road then climbs up the west slope of Willoughby Ridge into old growth forests of western hemlock and Pacific silver fir that have been fragmented by logging over the last thirty years. Montane forests of Pacific silver fir occupy a wide band between 1,000 and 3,000 feet in the western Olympics. This is one of the best locations on the Olympic Peninsula for eye-level views of Blue Grouse, Vaux's Swift, and Red Crossbill. Booming Blue Grouse are a common sight from mid-April through June and can often be closely approached with a vehicle. This can also be a good place to see and hear a Marbled Murrelet, at dawn, returning to its nesting area in the top of the old growth trees. Occasional pullouts offer unsurpassed views of the Hoh River Valley, the peaks of the Olympic Mountains, and the Pacific Ocean in the distance. At night, listen for calling Great Horned, Northern Pygmy, Northern Saw-whet, and, if lucky, Spotted Owls.

Look for pullouts with good views of the canopy of the downhill trees or clear cuts with views of old growth stands below the road. Traffic along the road is minimal since logging in the area was halted in an effort to protect the remaining old growth forests. For safety sake, pull to the shoulder of the road when birds are sighted.

About 7.3 miles from US 101, Forest Road H3160 goes off to the right. Continue along H3200 another 3.8 miles to the end of the road and a turn-around. This section of H3200 progresses through old growth forests and offers great views of Mt. Olympus, the inner Olympic Mountains, as well as Destruction Island and the ocean.

Return to US 101 via H3200. For those with a more adventurous spirit, take Forest Road H3160 to the left (a.k.a. Goat Trail). H3160 switchbacks down the hillside to arrive at Forest Road H3100 in about three miles. Use low gear and avoid riding the brakes - proceed slowly down this steep, winding road. These roads receive regular maintenance, but their condition can vary based on weather and/or logging activity. They may be impassable for weeks to months at a time, especially in winter. There are spectacular views from this road. Turn left onto H3100, go 1.4 miles, and turn right onto H3700, which in 0.4 miles enters the Upper Hoh Road. Turn right to return to US 101 (about 6½ miles) or left (about 6 miles) to the Hoh River entrance to the Olympic National Park.

Hoh Rain Forest

Hoh Rain Forest   Olympic National Park

At MP 178.5 on US 101, turn left onto the Upper Hoh Road to reach the visitor center, campground, and interpretive trails of the **Olympic National Park Hoh Rain Forest**. Stop at a pullout alongside any open area and scan the skies for Vaux's Swift (May through July). Willow Flycatcher, Hutton's Vireo, Swainson's Thrush, Orange-crowned and Wilson's Warblers, and Spotted Towhee sing in the clear cuts in the spring and summer. Keep a lookout for Merlin throughout the Hoh River valley.

Proceed 12.5 miles to the entrance to the Olympic National Park. Along the way, pass through various phases of managed forests from recent harvests to mature stands of western hemlock and western red cedar. There are many opportunities to pull over to look and listen for Hairy Woodpecker, Pacific-slope Flycatcher (summer), Chestnut-backed Chickadee, Brown Creeper (with its high-pitched song, April through July), Winter Wren, Golden-crowned Kinglet, and Varied Thrush.

Stop at the parking lot on the right just before the entrance to the national park and bird the **alder grove**. This grove contains Downy Woodpecker, Hammond's Flycatcher (conspicuous), Black-capped Chickadee, Warbling Vireo, and Black-throated

Gray Warbler, which are common in May through July.

Across the road and a few hundred feet west, a footbridge crosses a bog and a trail leads into conifers that host Hairy Woodpecker, Pacific-slope Flycatcher, Chestnut-backed Chickadee, and Brown Creeper from mid-May through mid-July.

Continue past the Registration Booth (fee) to the **Visitor Center** (about another 6 miles)

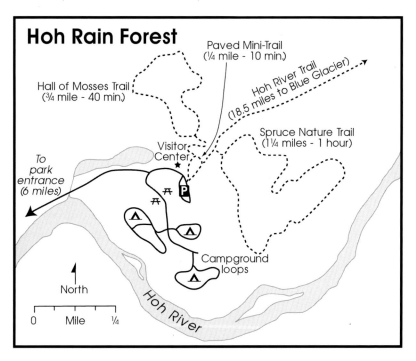

The **pond** by the Visitor Center may hold Green-winged Teal, Ring-necked Duck, Hooded Merganser, or Ruddy Duck with Great Blue Heron and Roosevelt Elk around the edges.

In the nearby **campground**, search for Gray and Steller's Jays and Northwestern Crow, which has moved into this area from its traditional location along the coast. Barred Owl may call at night in the spring.

The Visitor Center has rain forest exhibits and summer naturalist programs.

There are several self-guided nature trails to observe North

America's finest temperate rain forest. From the Visitor Center parking lot, take one of the several loop trails, such as the ³/₄ mile **Hall of Mosses Trail** or the 1¹/₄ mile **Spruce Nature Trail** with their moss-draped maples, to study classic rain forest habitat. Temperate rain forests ecosystems are rare throughout the world and require moderate temperatures, fog, and lots of rain—over 140 inches per year. The dominant rain forest species here are Sitka spruce, western hemlock, Douglas fir, western red cedar, bigleaf maple, red alder, vine maple, and black cottonwood. Mosses, lichens, and ferns (including licorice and sword fern) are abundant throughout these wet forests.

Hoh Rain Forest   Olympic National Park

The **Hoh River Trail** leaves from here and allows access into the alpine meadows of the **high country of the Olympic Mountains** reaching Blue Glacier in 18.5 miles. This trail is one of the most beautiful trails in the United States and one hiking magazine even voted it the second most beautiful trail in the world! The Hoh River Trail is the main route for those climbing Mt. Olympus and the best coastal access to the alpine meadows of the high country. More information on this trail is provided in Spring and Manning's *100 Hikes in Washington's South Cascades and Olympics.*

Mt. Olympus   Olympic National Park

Three days should be allowed for this pack back trip that meanders on the level through the multi-storied rain forest which harbors ferns, mosses, lichens, and liverworts and abundant growths of vine maple, huckleberry, red elderberry, and salmonberry. Watch for American Dipper along the upper stretches of the river. Look and listen for Western Screech, Northern Pygmy, and Northern Saw-whet Owls in the mature coniferous or mixed coniferous/deciduous woods. At about 13 miles, the trail leaves the Hoh valley and starts to climb. Near the end of the trail (17 miles) at 4,200 feet, dense groves of subalpine fir and mountain hemlock are encountered just before the open alpine meadows and the snout of Blue Glacier.

In the alpine habitat, expect to see similar birds as may be more easily accessed at Hurricane Ridge, such as Northern Goshawk, Golden Eagle, Merlin, Peregrine Falcon, Blue Grouse, Vaux's Swift, Northern Flicker, Olive-sided Flycatcher, Gray Jay, Common Raven, Townsend's Solitaire, Hermit Thrush, American Pipit, Dark-eyed Junco, Gray-crowned Rosy-Finch, Pine Grosbeak, and Red Crossbill.

Kalaloch Area

Continue south on US 101 to picturesque **Ruby Beach** (MP 164.7), with its mixture of sea stacks, tide pools, and sandy and rocky shores that are typical of this part of the coast. The name of the beach is derived from its garnet-colored sand. Check for Wandering Tattler (spring and fall), Black Turnstone, and Surfbird on nearby rocks and look for cormorants, Common Murre, and Pigeon Guillemot on Abbey Island.

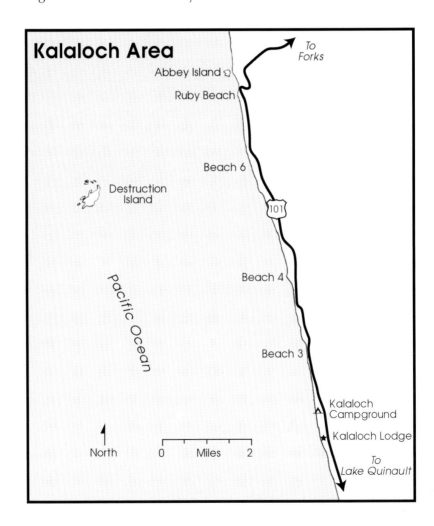

Kalaloch Area

To Forks

Abbey Island

Ruby Beach

Beach 6

Destruction Island

101

Beach 4

Pacific Ocean

Beach 3

Kalaloch Campground

Kalaloch Lodge

To Lake Quinault

North   0   Miles   2

At MP 163.4, a pullout on the right affords a view of **Destruction Island**, 4 miles offshore. Here a lighthouse built in 1891 stands guard over nesting colonies of Leach's Storm-petrel, Brandt's Cormorant, Western, Glaucous-winged, and the more common Glaucous-winged X Western Gulls, Common Murre, Pigeon Guillemot, Rhinoceros Auklet, and Tufted Puffin.

A series of six **beach accesses** are located along US 101 over the next few miles. Birders can expect to see shorebirds in season and roosting gulls as well as a number of people on weekends especially during summer. At MP 162.7 an unmarked road to the right ends at a high bluff with commanding views of Beach 6, Destruction Island, and the open ocean. At MP 160.4, Beach 4 has both a sandy and rocky beach with dramatic surf and tidal pools with barnacles, sea stars, sea anemones, and small crabs among the rocks. At MP 159.8 a path leads down to Beach 3.

Another pull off at MP 158.5 offers opportunities to scan the ocean for Gray Whales (April), passing Sooty Shearwater (summer and fall) and alcids. Scoters, Bald Eagle, Peregrine Falcon, Harbor Seal, and Sea Otter may occasionally be seen from these vantage points.

At MP 157.7, the Kalaloch Campground (pronounced "Clay-lock") offers tent and RV campsites and overlooks the Pacific Ocean. Because of its location, it is one of the most popular campgrounds in the Olympic National Park.

Razor clam diggers seem to have good success on the sandy beaches of the Kalaloch area during the lowest tides of winter.

At MP 157.1, the **Kalaloch Lodge** (360-962-2271) sits on a bluff above the Kalaloch Creek where it enters the ocean. Bathing gulls in the freshwater creek may include Heermann's (summer and fall), Ring-billed, California, Western, Glaucous-winged, Glaucous-winged X Western hybrid, and later in the fall and winter Mew, Herring, and Thayer's (rare). Coastal spruce forests intermixed with shrubby thickets surround the lodge. The thickets host Orange-crowned and Wilson's

Warblers, and the "Sooty" race of the Fox Sparrow. Swallows dart around the lodge hawking insects in summer. The sandy beach has shorebirds in migration with offshore loons, grebes, and scoters. The facilities include a restaurant and accommodations in the lodge, a number of waterfront cabins, and a convenience store with a gas pump.

Kalaloch River mouth at Kalaloch Lodge   Bob Morse

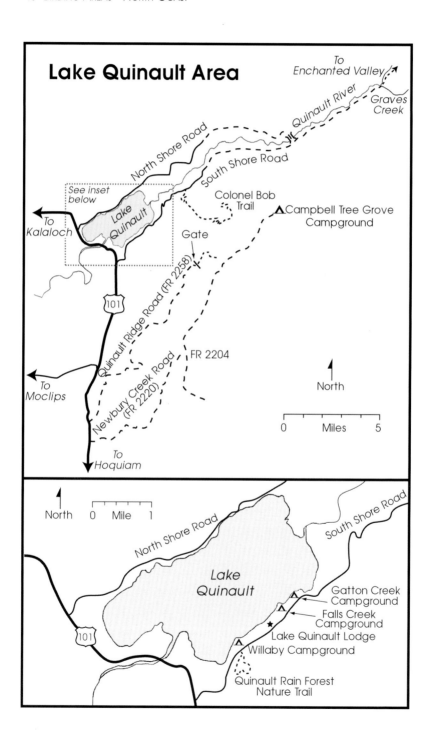

Lake Quinault Area

To Enchanted Valley

Quinault River

Graves Creek

North Shore Road

South Shore Road

See inset below

To Kalaloch

Lake Quinault

Colonel Bob Trail

▲ Campbell Tree Grove Campground

Gate

To Moclips

Quinault Ridge Road (FR 2258)

Newbury Creek Road (FR 2220)

FR 2204

North

0   Miles   5

To Hoquiam

North   0   Mile   1

North Shore Road

South Shore Road

Lake Quinault

Gatton Creek Campground

Falls Creek Campground

Lake Quinault Lodge

Willaby Campground

Quinault Rain Forest Nature Trail

Lake Quinault

Lake Quinault, a four-mile long freshwater lake fed by Olympic Mountain glaciers, lies in the southwest corner of the Olympic National Park. It is bordered on the south by the rugged Olympic National Forest and on the north by the pristine Olympic National Park. Its miles of adjoining dense conifers, lush broadleaf forests, lakeside shrubby thickets, and open fresh water provide a number of opportunities to sample the birding in this part of the Olympic peninsula. Much of the better birding is along the south shore of Lake Quinault.

At MP 125.6, turn left onto the **Lake Quinault South Shore Road.** 1.4 miles from US 101, turn right into the parking lot for the **Quinault Rain Forest Nature Trail**. Take time to enjoy this self-guided ½ mile tour of a native forest with its richly vegetated undergrowth of ferns, moss, and lichens. A Northwest Forest Pass is required to park at the trailhead but the interpretive signs along the trail are exceptional and the tour is worth the time and money. (A pass may be acquired at the self-service pay station here or at the Lake Quinault National Forest Service Ranger Station near the Lake Quinault Lodge). A 400-year Douglas fir towers over the trail near the gorge. Expect to see Black-capped and Chestnut-backed Chickadees, Winter Wren, Varied Thrush, and Dark-eyed Junco. In the scenic gorge with its cascading stream, search for American Dipper as well as Merlin (rare in summer). An active Osprey nest is located a short distance from the nature trail up the Quinault Loop Trail (see Lake Quinault South Shore map). Marbled Murrelet has been heard and seen, at dawn, returning to their nest sites in the mature trees near the Willaby Creek Trail.

There are three forest service campgrounds along the South Shore Road (closed in winter), a few restaurants, cabins, convenience store, and a gas station.

The **Lake Quinault Lodge**, built in 1926, stands as a majestic reminder of the old lodges built in the national parks and forests in the 1920s and 1930s. With its rustic style, expansive grounds, and dining room with a spectacular view of the lake, it is a "must see" for birders visiting the area.

Lake Quinault South Shore

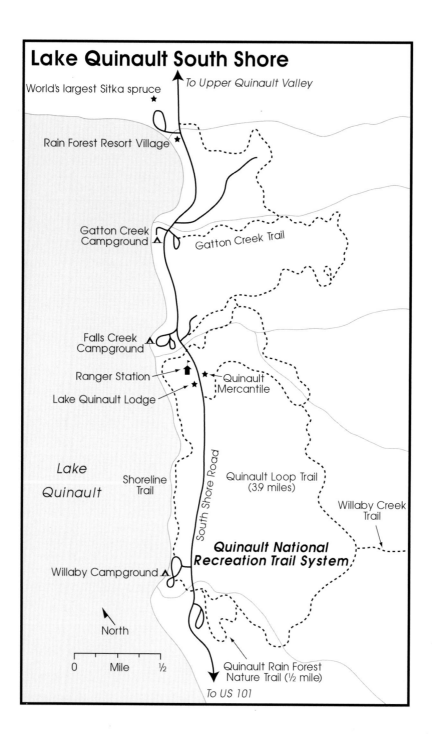

World's largest Sitka spruce ★

To Upper Quinault Valley

Rain Forest Resort Village ★

Gatton Creek Campground ⛺

Gatton Creek Trail

Falls Creek Campground ⛺

Ranger Station

Quinault Mercantile ★

Lake Quinault Lodge ★

Lake

Quinault

Shoreline Trail

South Shore Road

Quinault Loop Trail (3.9 miles)

Willaby Creek Trail

Quinault National Recreation Trail System

Willaby Campground ⛺

North

0   Mile   ½

Quinault Rain Forest Nature Trail (½ mile)

To US 101

The **Quinault National Recreation Trail System**, starting across the road from the lodge, offers a series of hiking trails through towering coniferous forests. There is also a shoreline trail passing through broadleaf forests and shrubby thickets along the lake.

Birds of the coniferous forest here include Blue Grouse, Marbled Murrelet (seen at dawn returning to nest sites at the top of old growth trees), Spotted and Northern Saw-whet Owls, Hairy and Pileated Woodpeckers, Steller's Jay, Common Raven, Chestnut-backed Chickadee, Red-breasted Nuthatch, Brown Creeper, Winter Wren, both kinglets, Varied Thrush, Townsend's Warbler (uncommon in fall and winter), and Dark-eyed Junco. Don't expect to see all these birds on one trip along the trail.

Check around the lodge, other lakeside buildings, gardens, shrubby thickets, broadleaf forests, and along the shoreline trail for Red-breasted Sapsucker, Downy Woodpecker, Northern Flicker, Olive-sided and Pacific-slope Flycatchers, Hutton's and Warbling Vireos, swallows, Swainson's Thrush, Orange-crowned, Yellow, Black-throated Gray, and Wilson's Warblers, Common Yellowthroat, Western Tanager, Black-headed Grosbeak, "Sooty" Fox (winter), and White-crowned Sparrows.

Lake Quinault hosts Common Loon, Common and Hooded Mergansers, wintering Trumpeter Swan, and occasional Marbled Murrelet (summer) which nest in the old growth trees in the surrounding hills. This is one of the few locations where the murrelet is regularly seen on fresh water. Around the lake, check for Bald Eagles (especially in winter), Osprey nests in snags, and American Dipper may be seen along the lakeshore and in streams entering the lake, especially in winter at the east end.

Just east of the lodge is the Quinault Ranger Station, which provides trail, maps, a local bird list, and Northwest Forest Passes.

A mile farther east along the South Shore Road is the **Rain Forest Resort Village** (motel, cabins, restaurant, and RV park). At the end of the cabin loop road, near the lake, stands the world's largest Sitka spruce tree, measuring 58 feet in circumference and 191 feet tall. Nearby, a freshwater marsh crossed by a footbridge may be worth checking. Common Snipe have been seen along the shore below and to the west of the restaurant and Trumpeter Swan winter in this end of the lake.

Lake Quinault   Bob Morse

The South Shore Road continues east and then leaves the lakeshore to meander through open farmlands bordered by moss-draped alders and maples into the Upper Quinault Valley. In the winter, these fields may host a herd of Roosevelt Elk.

In less than three miles, the trailhead to the steep **Colonel Bob** Trail is on the right (Northwest Forest Pass required to park here). Spotted Owl has been heard and seen along this trail in the past. It is important to recognize that these birds are threatened with extinction and already subject to disturbances during legitimate studies to aid their conservation. The playing of tapes is discouraged. Spotted Owls call from the neighboring hillsides, especially from April through July.

Within two more miles, the South Shore Road becomes a dirt road and eventually the road parallels the **Quinault River**. About a mile after the road enters the Olympic National Park, the road crosses over a bridge, joining the North Shore Road to form a loop around Lake Quinault. The dirt portion of the road is 12 miles in length, dusty in summer, poorly maintained, not advised for passenger vehicles, and may not be passable in winter. A convenient turnaround is at the end of the paved section of the South Shore Road.

If the birder were to continue up the South Shore Road, they might find Harlequin Duck which breed further up the Quinault River, from the Graves Creek Ranger Station up to Enchanted Valley, a stretch of about 13 miles. The road ends at Graves Creek (or sooner if the road needs repair). The rest of the trip is on foot along the Enchanted Valley Trail. Search for Harlequin Duck, especially in spring and summer, along the Quinault River up to Graves Creek. Watch for large numbers of Bald Eagles feeding on dead salmon in January along the river and creeks.

After completing the exploration of the birding spots along the South Shore Road, return to US 101 and go left (south).

Quinault Ridge Road
(See Lake Quinault Area map)

At MP 118.2 on US 101, just north of the Olympic National Forest boundary, turn left on the **Quinault Ridge Road** (Forest Service Road FR2258). After leaving the highway the road ascends one mile to an intersection with other logging roads. Stay left. The road continues approximately 6 miles through western hemlock and western red cedar to where a gate blocks the road. This road is subject to washouts and may be closed before the gate. Watch for hidden potholes on the flat sections of the road. Evidence of patches of old growth forest is viewed from this road with views of Lake Quinault to the north.

The road can be productive in late spring through early fall (before deer hunting season). Beyond the gate the road can be quite good for nesting species including Northern Goshawk (rare), Ruffed and Blue Grouse, Gray Jay, and Hermit Thrush. Fall migration can be good for Turkey Vulture, raptors that include all three accipiters, and Golden Eagle. A two-mile walk from the gate towards the immediate end of Quinault Ridge Road provides views of the higher peaks of the central and northern Olympic Range to the east. Birds to listen and look for include Band-tailed Pigeon (fall migrant), Red-breasted Sapsucker, five species of flycatchers (including Hammond's), Cassin's Vireo, Townsend's Solitaire, MacGillivray's Warbler, "Sooty" Fox Sparrow, and possibly Pine Grosbeak (to be looked for in late summer-fall, after breeding dispersal from the higher elevations).

The Quinault Ridge Road has been a good place to find Townsend's Warbler in early fall.

After the first mile from US 101, in evening listen for Western Screech (lower elevations), Great Horned, Northern Pygmy, Spotted, Barred, and Northern Saw-whet Owls.

Campbell Tree Grove
(See Lake Quinault Area map)

One of the most accessible Marbled Murrelet nesting locations along the coast is in the **Campbell Tree Grove** USFS campground east of US 101. Murrelets are active at dawn from May through August at their nest sites. To make this side trip, turn south on US 101 to the Newbury Creek Road, (MP 117.1), also known as FR 2220 and turn left (east). It is 19 miles to the Campbell Tree Grove on a graded dirt road (watch for potholes) and takes about one hour from US 101. A Northwest Forest Pass is required to park at the campground. See More Coastal Information Appendix for information on obtaining a Forest Pass.

FR 2220 travels through managed forests of western red cedar and western hemlock with occasional clear cuts and stands of broadleaf forests and shrubby thickets in the creek bottoms. At 9 miles, go left on FR 2204 and follow this road another 10 miles to the campground.

The Campbell Tree Grove campground, located in an old growth forest predominantly of western hemlock along the Humptulips River, is only open for camping in summer. Thanks to surveys by biologist Janet Anthony, it is known that Marbled Murrelet nest in the upper canopy of the old growth trees in the campground and are active in the predawn, especially in July, flying to and from their nest sites to the Pacific Ocean. They often make their characteristic " Keeer" call as they fly above the treetops (somewhat like a Northern Flicker or distant gull call). The noise their wings make as they power dive into the tree tops sounds like a jet engine, according to Anthony, although this is a rare event to witness.

This site is within three miles of Colonel Bob, so Spotted Owls should be listened for from April through July.

Return to US 101 via FR 2204 and FR 2220.

Taholah, Cape Elizabeth, and Point Grenville

Go north on US 101 about three miles. At MP 120.1, go west on the Moclips Highway to get to Taholah, a small village that is home to the Quinault Indian Nation. The Moclips Highway is a 20-mile stretch of road including 5 miles of graded dirt road through areas of lodgepole pine, Douglas fir, and red alder. At the "T" intersection with SR 109, turn right. The north end of SR 109 ends just outside Taholah. Go left (west) to Taholah.

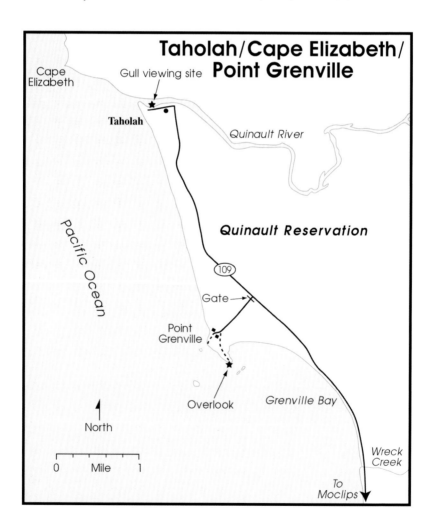

The town of **Taholah** and surrounding Indian lands are situated in thick, wet, coastal coniferous forests. In the town of Taholah, go right at the first stop sign (5th Street), then left onto Quinault Street. When the Indians are fishing in the Quinault River or when the Quinault Pride Seafood fish processing plant is operating (Monday-Friday), there is plenty of food for foraging gulls. Glaucous-winged, Western, and Glaucous-winged X Western hybrid gulls are most common but search for Franklin (fall, rare), Mew (fall through spring), Ring-billed, California (fall), Herring (fall through spring), and Thayer's (rare, winter). Bald Eagles often perch in the tall conifers lining the river. Quinault Pride Seafood sells Blueback Salmon (spawns exclusively in the Quinault River), smoked salmon, and canned seafood.

Looking at tidepools at Cape Elizabeth   Bob Morse

Cape Elizabeth, along the coast a short distance north of Taholah, is situated among old growth and second growth forests of the Quinault Indian Nation. This isolated promontory of land and surrounding tide pools is only accessible during very low tides. It is off limits to visitors except by private invitation and a guided tour led by a Quinault Indian Nation member. Contact the Grays Harbor Audubon Society for information on tours to Cape Elizabeth during low summer tides.

Tidepool   Olympic National Park

South of Taholah, at MP 37.7 on SR 109, is the entrance to **Point Grenville**. The access road is a paved, one-lane road to the west but a locked gate restricts access. To gain access to Point Grenville, make arrangements ahead of time with Mike Mail of the Quinault Indian Nation (home phone: 360-276-4315) or with the Quinault Indian Nation Natural Resources Department (360-276-8211). A donation of $5.00 per person is customary. All birder contributions are used to support tribal youth recreational activities.

During its years of military use, the area around the buildings at Point Grenville was cleared and lawns planted. Since the facility was abandoned in the 1970s, the fields have reverted to tall grass interspersed with shrubby thickets.

Migrant songbirds use the wax myrtle, other bushes, and forest edges. The "Sooty" Fox Sparrow has its most southern known nesting location here and is most easily found in the winter in bushes to the southwest of the buildings.

Point Grenville is reached by following the paved road from the gate to the spot where old, dilapidated military buildings stand. Unfortunately, logging has left only a narrow corridor of mixed coniferous and broadleaf forest habitat along the entrance road. Even so, Blue Grouse nest here, Common Ravens patrol overhead, and Pileated Woodpeckers call from these woods. Park by the abandoned buildings. Walk north, then west on a dirt track across an open field leading to an overlook facing west. In the past, Tufted Puffins have nested in the grassy bluff just below the overlook across from the offshore haystack. The number of Tufted Puffin currently nesting here is uncertain. Pigeon Guillemot nest in the rock cliffs to the north and Pelagic Cormorant nest on the white-washed, open cliff ledges to the south. On the offshore rock formations, Western, Glaucous-winged, and Glaucous-winged X Western Gulls nest in the grassy areas near the top, while Pelagic Cormorant and Common Murre build nests on the exposed cliff faces. Peregrine Falcon may be visible on these rocks or hunting nearby.

Islet west of Pt. Grenville   Bob Morse

A second viewing area requires a short walk along a tangled wooded trail of red alder, huckleberry, and salal to the south side of the point. From the old buildings follow a dirt road to the southwest. Where it appears to end, a small trail leads into the brush. This trail ends at a steep **overlook**. Black Oystercatchers are normally seen on the rocks below or on the rocks just offshore. This may be the most reliable spot to find this species along the entire coast. The islets to the south have nesting Pelagic Cormorant, gulls, as well as Tufted Puffin, on the furthest islet to the left. The waters below have Western Grebe, Pelagic Cormorant, Surf and White-winged Scoters, Common Murre, Pigeon Guillemot, and passing loons.

Islets south of Pt. Grenville (Tufted   Bob Morse
Puffins nest on top of far left islet)

Depending on tides, time of year, and weather, birding at Point Grenville can be outstanding to dreary. It is at its best in May or early June, but other seasons offer good birding potential as well. Point Grenville can be a great migrant trap and is almost always an excellent sea-watch location. Uncommon or rare birds such as Northern Fulmar, Horned Puffin, Palm Warbler, Vesper, Lark, and Black-throated Sparrows, and Chestnut-collared

Longspur have been seen here. One fall morning a Virginia Rail and a Mourning Dove were seen within a few feet of each other. During migration, Gray Whales, seabirds and waterfowl pass the tip in good numbers. The scenic beauty of the point makes the trip a success no matter what birds are seen or missed.

Two and a half miles further south on SR 109, fresh water **Wreck Creek** empties into the ocean. Bathing gulls and shorebirds are sometimes on the sandy shore and Bald Eagle may be perched in nearby trees. A parking pullout is near the bridge.

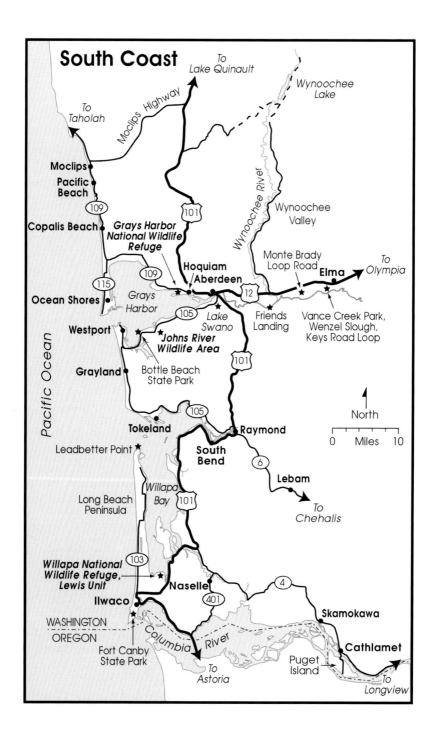

South Coast

To Lake Quinault

Wynoochee Lake

Moclips Highway

To Taholah

Moclips

Pacific Beach

109

Copalis Beach

Grays Harbor National Wildlife Refuge

Wynoochee River

101

Wynoochee Valley

Monte Brady Loop Road

To Olympia

Elma

109

115

Hoquiam

Aberdeen

12

Ocean Shores

Grays Harbor

105

Lake Swano

Friends Landing

Vance Creek Park, Wenzel Slough, Keys Road Loop

Westport

Johns River Wildlife Area

Grayland

Bottle Beach State Park

101

Pacific Ocean

105

North

0   Miles   10

Tokeland

Raymond

Leadbetter Point

South Bend

6

Lebam

Willapa Bay

101

Long Beach Peninsula

To Chehalis

103

Willapa National Wildlife Refuge, Lewis Unit

Naselle

401

4

Ilwaco

Skamokawa

WASHINGTON

OREGON

Columbia River

Fort Canby State Park

To Astoria

Puget Island

Cathlamet

To Longview

SOUTH COAST

The South Coast starts south of Point Grenville where the rocky cliffs give way to open beaches, expansive mud flats, and salt marshes.

Moclips to Ocean City

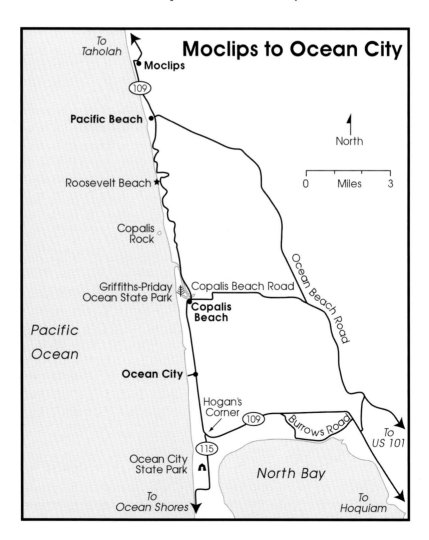

Continue south on SR 109, and in the town of Moclips, take Second Street west to gain access to the sandy beach. 100 years ago, Moclips was the terminus for excursion trains which ran daily between Seattle and this popular ocean front destination. If the tide is out, drive south for 1½ miles to **Pacific Beach**. Be careful not to drive too close to the water or too far up on the beach; it is easy to get stuck in the soft sand. Following existing tire tracks in the sand is usually safe.

Shorebirds and gulls may be on this quiet stretch of beach. At the end of 1½ miles, proceed up the access road, go straight through two stop signs, and then go right onto SR 109.

At the four-way stop on SR 109 at Pacific Beach, birders may go south along SR 109 or detour east on the Ocean Beach Road to reach Copalis Beach.

The **Ocean Beach Road** route during the spring can be quite good, as many of the resident and migrant songbirds such as chickadees, Bewick's and Winter Wrens, Orange-crowned, Yellow-rumped, and Wilson's Warblers are singing and relatively easy to find. In other seasons expect fewer species to be heard. Tall second-growth stands of Douglas fir are near the road, and all stages of forest regeneration can be accessed easily by following dirt tracks a short distance off the main road. The variety of habitat (coniferous forests, stands of red alder, and shrubby thickets), infrequent traffic, and ease of parking make this route desirable for anyone who might choose to 'bird along the way.'

After eight miles from the four-way stop at Pacific Beach, a right turn onto the Copalis Beach Road brings the birder back to Copalis Beach on the coast.

The more direct route to Copalis Beach is to take SR 109 south from Pacific Beach, although it is difficult to stop for birding along this twisting, narrow, coastal road with few pullouts. Taking the access road to **Roosevelt Beach** provides an opportunity to drive south along the beach for one mile to check for gulls and shorebirds and marvel at how wind has shaped the oceanfront trees along this part of the coast. Return to SR 109 via the same access road. At Iron Springs Resort, there is limited beach access. Black Oystercatcher use **Copalis Rock**, a large rock promontory, $1/2$ mile south and several hundred yards offshore. Cross the creek and walk south along the beach to view the rock. A scope is a must.

Continue south on SR 109 to Copalis Beach, which was once headquarters for local canneries that packaged and sold razor clams.

Go west on Benner Road to the **Griffiths-Priday Ocean State Park** (day use only). This open grass dune park offers restrooms and sheltered picnic areas. In the past (no recent records), Snowy Plovers have nested in the open dune areas. The nesting area is closed March 15 through August 31.

Ocean City is reached by going three miles farther south on SR 109.

In Ocean City, take a right (west) on Second Street to gain access to a wide, open beach. At low tide, it can be driven south past the Quinault Beach Resort and Casino about four miles to the Damon Road exit at the Best Western Motel in Ocean Shores or an additional $3/4$ mile to the Chance A La Mar exit next to the Shilo Inn. Once again, be careful not to drive too close to the water or too far up the beach where it is easy to get stuck in the soft sand.

Ocean Shores

Ocean Shores is arguably the best spot in Washington to watch birds. Close to 300 species of birds have been observed here. On any given day, whether on a wet winter day or one with bright sunshine, seeing a hundred species of birds is an attainable goal.

Ocean Shores is a thin six mile long peninsula laced with 23 miles of canals and lakes, bounded on the west by the Pacific Ocean and on the south and east by the waters of Grays Harbor.

Ocean Shores from the south   George E. Brooks

The reason for the large variety of birds is its location along the coast and its wide range of habitats: long sandy beaches, tidal salt marshes, rock jetty, extensive mudflats, sand dunes, fresh water ponds, woodlots, a golf course, marina, and even a sewage treatment plant. Nowhere else in Washington State do all these habitats coexist in one small place.

Ocean Shores is also a mecca for unusual and rare birds in Washington. It is one of the best spots in the lower forty-eight states to find Pacific Golden-Plover in fall. Mottled Petrel, Manx

Shearwater, Eurasian Dotterel, Bristle-thighed Curlew, Ivory Gull, Least Tern, Yellow Wagtail, and McKay's Bunting have each put in an appearance or two.

Ocean Shores is exciting birding at any time of year, but fall is particularly good, especially between late July and early October when migrating shorebirds pass through. They do not appear in the vast numbers of the spring migration that sees 250,000 or more shorebirds winging through Grays Harbor on their way to their nesting grounds in the arctic; but fall does provide a better variety. Pacific Golden-Plover appear from mid August to mid October and American Golden-Plover from mid September to mid October. Baird's Sandpiper appear from early August to early October and Pectoral Sandpiper occur from early September to mid October with a few appearing in early August. Starting in late September, Sharp-tailed Sandpiper is occasionally found in the *Salicornia* marsh in the Game Range (often with Pectoral Sandpiper) and, by early October, small numbers of Rock Sandpiper reappear to spend the winter on the jetty. Parasitic and Pomarine Jaegers are regularly seen from the jetty as they harass the flocks of migrating Common Terns in fall.

Ocean Shores can be reached by continuing south on Highway 109 to Hogan's Corner, which is the intersection of SR 109 and SR 115. Turn south on SR 115 toward Ocean Shores.

Ocean City State Park, on the west side of SR 115, offers good birding. The coniferous and broadleaf trees and shrubby thickets throughout the park usually contain Downy Woodpecker, Cassin's and Hutton's Vireos, Black-capped and Chestnut-backed Chickadees, Bushtit, Brown Creeper, Bewick's and Winter Wrens, Varied Thrush (winter), and nesting Olive-sided Flycatcher. Both the Audubon and Myrtle race of the Yellow-rumped Warbler appear here with Myrtle more common in winter. Check for Orange-crowned, Black-throated Gray (spring to fall), Townsend's (fall), and Wilson's Warblers, Spotted Towhee, "Sooty" Fox Sparrow (winter), Song and Golden-crowned Sparrow (latter, winter), Dark-eyed Junco, and Purple Finch.

There are freshwater ponds along both sides of the entrance road into the park. A parking area is situated just beyond the ponds, on the right. Check the ponds for Pied-billed Grebe, Great Egret (rare, summer and fall), Green Heron (late spring and summer), Wood Duck, Hooded Merganser, Sora (summer), and yellowlegs (in migration). American Bittern and Virginia Rail have nested here. Trumpeter or Tundra Swans may be present in winter.

A small parking area on the right is located 0.1 mile past the Registration Office inside the State Park. From here an unmarked trail leads through the trees to a freshwater pond and swamp where American Bittern, Virginia Rail, Sora, Marsh Wren, and Common Yellowthroat (summer) may be found.

Drive to the parking area for the beach and check the nearby wet areas for Solitary (very rare), Pectoral (fall), and Sharp-tailed (rare, fall) Sandpipers and the willows for passerines.

Return to SR 115.

A short distance (0.1 mile) south of the park entrance along SR 115 is a hidden road on the right blocked by a white gate that leads to the State Parks sewage pond. The small pond is on the right at the end of the road. Wood Duck are sometimes here in summer. Chestnut-backed Chickadee and Golden-crowned Kinglet are resident and Red-breasted Nuthatch forage in the surrounding woods in winter.

Ocean Shores beach   George E. Brooks

A wide, hard packed, six mile-long, sandy **ocean beach** lies along the western edge of Ocean Shores. The beach can be reached by car from any of five entrance roads (see map).

During spring and fall migration, large mixed-species flocks of shorebirds are common along the beach especially at high tide. Carefully check all the shorebirds. Bristle-thighed Curlews were seen here in May 1998 and a Curlew Sandpiper in early September 1997.

The beach is good for close studies of gulls including Heermann's (July to October, summer best), Mew (September to May), Ring-billed, California (fall), Herring (fall through spring, uncommon), Thayer's (winter, rare), Western, Glaucous-winged, Glaucous-winged X Western hybrid, and Glaucous (winter, rare) Gulls. Offshore, Brown Pelican (mid May to early November), gulls, and migrating Sooty Shearwater (July to October) may be visible.

The speed limit on the beach is 25 mph, and parts of the beach may be closed to vehicular traffic (it is illegal to drive over the razor clam beds exposed at low tide). Please observe these closures and speeds and avoid driving too far up the beach where it is possible to get stuck in the soft sand. If that occurs, the best solution is to let most of the air out the tires and then try to drive out. If that doesn't work - call a tow truck.

Godwits and dowitchers on
Ocean Shores golf course

Jeff Skriletz

If undisturbed by golfers, any of the grassy expanses of the **Ocean Shores Golf Course** may host flocks of Canada and occasional Greater White-fronted and Snow Geese, ducks and shorebirds. Flocks of American Wigeon, with an occasional Eurasian Wigeon, winter here. Buff-Breasted Sandpiper may rest here during fall storms. Solitary and Sharp-tailed Sandpipers have been found in the ditch along the fairways behind Linde's Landing.

Most of the golf course is easily viewed from neighboring roads. Three of the better vantage points are along Point Brown Avenue, Ocean Shores Boulevard, and Minard Avenue south of W. Chance A La Mer.

Generally, golf course birding is best early in the morning, during high tides, or during stormy weather. At these times, the golf course may be the best place to find golden-plovers, godwits, and curlews.

Drive south on Ocean Shores Boulevard to reach the **Point Brown Jetty**.

NOTE: The streets of Ocean Shores are currently under repair and may, in some areas, be in bad condition. Point Brown Avenue has been repaired, is in good condition, and provides a good way to reach the southern end of Ocean Shores.

Ocean Shores jetty   George E. Brooks

Wear warm clothing when birding the jetty during the fall, winter, or spring. Be aware of tide conditions. At high tides or when there are big swells, waves can break over the top. Avoid the jetty at this time.

From the beach on the north side of the jetty, scan the breakwater rocks for Double-crested, Brandt's, and Pelagic Cormorants, Wandering Tattler (mid April through May, late July through mid October), Black Turnstone (mid July through May), Surfbird (late July through April), Rock Sandpiper (early October through mid April), and Mew (September to May), Herring (September to May), Western, and Glaucous-winged Gulls. The shorebirds are often seen on the rocks close to shore on an incoming tide. A scope is helpful. Walking out on the rock jetty (treacherous) may be necessary to get good views of the rock shorebirds.

From the top of the jetty, scan south and west across the **channel** and ocean for passing Red-throated, Pacific, and Common Loons, Sooty Shearwater (summer and fall), Brown Pelican (summer through fall), cormorants, Surf and White-winged Scoters, Heermann's Gull (summer and fall), Black-legged Kittiwake (fall through spring), Caspian Tern (spring through fall), Common Murre, and Rhinoceros Auklet. Visit the jetty in the morning to avoid the glare of the afternoon sun.

Channel between Ocean Shores   Keith Brady
and Westport

Migrating flocks of Common Tern (May and mid-August through mid-September) often attract a Parasitic Jaeger.

Gray Whale migrate off the coast and are sometimes visible especially during their migration, from March through May. Harbor Seal and California Sea Lion are common in waters off the jetty.

Manx Shearwaters have been seen in the channel between the jetty and Westport in late summer and fall. Other species rarely seen from the jetty include Short-tailed Shearwater, Northern Fulmar, Mottled Petrel, Pink-footed Shearwater, Fork-tailed Storm-Petrel, Sabine's Gull, Cassin's Auklet, and Horned Puffin.

The sandy area with its short beach grass between East Ocean Shores Boulevard and the rock wall south and east of the Atlantic Avenue Condominium in the fall and winter have had Horned Lark, Lapland Longspur, and Snow Bunting. Bristle-thighed Curlews were seen nearby in May 1998.

The **Ocean Shores Sewage Treatment Plant**, located further east on Ocean Shores Boulevard, is open to the public from 8:30 a.m. to 4:30 p.m., Monday through Friday.

The three sewer treatment ponds provide shelter during storms as well as a high tide refuge for ducks, shorebirds, and gulls. A Yellow Wagtail visited one foggy day in July 1992. Scope the vegetated edges of the ponds closely for shorebirds, especially at high tide. Sharp-tailed Sandpipers have been seen here in fall, and Red Phalaropes may be in the ponds after winter storms.

A McKay's Bunting wintered just outside the plant in 1988 with a flock of Snow Buntings. Lapland Longspur can usually be found from mid-September to mid-November in the short grass between the sewage treatment plant fence and the channel between Ocean Shores and Westport.

Paths along the south and north sides of the sewage treatment plant fence provide access to the tidal mudflats and *Salicornia* marshes of the Washington State Department of Fish and Wildlife Area (a.k.a., the **Game Range**). Park off Ocean Shores Boulevard near the fence. The path along the south side of the sewage treatment plant ends at the east end of the jetty. During high tide or with strong winds from the west, the rocks, beach, and bay here may have rock shorebirds, Elegant Tern (rare, summer), and alcids. In the bay search for Red-throated Loons and Black Scoters among the more numerous Surf and White-winged Scoters.

Pectoral and the rarer Sharp-tailed Sandpipers (latter, late September to late October) are most often seen in the *Salicornia* marsh east and north of the entrance paths into the Game Range. The best birding is one or two hours before or at high tide. Calf-high waterproof boots are suggested for walking in the wet *Salicornia* marsh.

Continue north on Ocean Shores Boulevard, which becomes Sportsman Street. Go right on Fairwood Drive, then left onto Marine View Drive, then right on Torrisdale Avenue to Cabana Pool on the right. Park behind the pool and take the nature trail around **Perkins Lake**, a small freshwater lake that hosts grebes, ducks, coot, and sometimes phalaropes, especially during stormy weather and migration. Brush surrounds much of the shoreline. A few Palm Warblers have been seen here, as well as the more common Northern Flicker, Black-capped Chickadee, Bushtit, Bewick's and Marsh Wrens, Yellow-rumped Warbler (fall to spring), Common Yellowthroat (summer), Spotted Towhee, "Sooty" Fox Sparrow (winter), Song and Golden-crowned Sparrows (fall through spring), and Dark-eyed Junco.

Return to Marine View Drive, go left and then take a right onto **Tonquin Avenue**. There is another access to the Game Range at the end of Tonquin Avenue. Walk around the gate and through an opening in the wax myrtle to the right of the building to get to the open salt marsh of the Game Range. One winter a Swamp Sparrow was seen near the logs just before the trail drops into the *Salicornia* marsh. This is perhaps the more difficult approach to the Game Range because of the deep salt water sloughs that cross this area. It can have its rewards, however, during a very high tide. One fall day in 1979, two Buff-breasted Sandpipers, three Ruffs, and a flock of over 20 golden-plovers were observed from this spot.

Return to Marine View Drive and go right. A small, open, grassy field adjacent to the **concrete water tower** along Marine View Drive provides a good view of Lake Minard. Walk down to the lake to watch grebes, ducks, and bathing gulls. This is a good place to get close views of Heermann's Gull in fall and Herring and Thayer's Gulls (rare) in winter. Red-necked Phalarope may be here in migration and Red Phalarope during or after severe winter storms. Resident Ring-necked Pheasant call from the tall grassy area to the east.

Across Marine View Drive from the tower, a pullout up a four-foot embankment provides a good view of the tidal mudflats and surrounding saltwater marshes of the east end of the Game Range. This spot is best on a rising or falling tide and early in the day to avoid glare from the sun. A scope is necessary for views of roosting Whimbrel, other shorebirds, gulls, and terns. A Bar-tailed Godwit has been observed from this spot in the fall.

Proceed east along Marine View Drive to reach the road to

Damon Point (a.k.a., Catala Spit), a mile-long spit of sand covered with beach grass extending east into Grays Harbor. It is the southeastern tip of Ocean Shores. Along Damon Point Road, there is a parking area located on the right, 0.4 of a mile from Marine View Drive. This is the entrance to the eastern end of the Game Range.

To access this part of the Game Range, park here and walk south along the path through the sand dunes and then west. A long narrow sand spit extends from this east end of the Game Range to the west.

NOTE: The Damon Point Road is subject to washouts when winter storms and high tides sweep over the road. If the road is closed, park near the restrooms at the beginning of the road and walk west around the Snowy Plover nesting area to gain access to the narrow sand spit of the Game Range.

Bird the sparsely vegetated flats and the water edges of the **Game Range sand spit** for Black-bellied Plover, both Pacific and American Golden-Plovers, Semipalmated Plover, yellowlegs, Whimbrel, Marbled Godwit, Red Knot, Western, Least and Baird's (fall, uncommon) Sandpipers, Dunlin, Buff-breasted Sandpiper (fall, rare), dowitchers, Horned Lark, American Pipit, and Lapland Longspur (fall). Parts of the spit may be closed from March 15 through August to accommodate the nesting Snowy Plover.

The saltwater bay on the south side of the sand spit typically hosts Red-throated Loon (a small number often summer here), Common Loon, Brown Pelican (spring through fall), cormorants, and all three species of scoters. Occasionally, Long-tailed Duck and jaegers may appear here. Rough-legged Hawk (winter), Merlin, Peregrine Falcon, and other raptors hunt the Game Range on a regular basis. Rarities do turn up: Yellow-billed Loon, Ross's and Emperor Geese, White-tailed Kite, Eurasian Dotterel (October 1999), Curlew Sandpiper, Ruff (rare fall migrant on the sand spit and in the *Salicornia* marsh), Little Gull, Elegant and Least Terns.

Return to the parking area and proceed toward the end of the **Damon Point Road**.

NOTE: If the road is closed, it may be necessary to walk around the south end of the Damon Point Pond to get to the tip of Damon Point.

The saltwater bay to the north of the Damon Point Road normally has Common Loon and Western Grebe. In the fall, Baird's Sandpiper may be found feeding along the high-tide kelp line. There is a picnic area along the water's edge.

Damon Point and Ocean Shores marina   George E. Brooks

Farther along the spit road, about 0.2 of a mile, the **Damon Point Pond**, a long, narrow pond on the right, attracts a variety of waterfowl. Its edges often host shorebirds at high tide. In fall this is a good place to check for Pacific and American Golden-Plovers, Baird's Sandpiper, and less regularly, Buff-breasted Sandpiper. In winter, Red Phalarope may be present. In late August and early September, the area around the pond is probably the most reliable spot along the Washington coast for Buff-breasted Sandpiper. Watch for Northern Shrike in winter in the vegetation around the pond or north of the Damon Point Road perched in short evergreen trees.

Snowy Plover have their northern-most nesting location in the United States at Ocean Shores. They nest in the area south and west of the pond. To protect this rare Washington nester, this area and other places on Damon Point and the Game Range are closed to access during the breeding season (15 March to 31 August each year). The nesting area is well marked with signs. The other areas of Damon Point are open for use year-round. Please respect the closure and avoid possible citations and fines.

The Damon Point Road ends in another 0.7 mile at a vantage point with nearby picnic tables—a great place for a picnic lunch. Set up a scope at the point and enjoy Red-throated, Pacific and Common Loons, Horned and Western Grebes (watch for Clark's), Brown Pelican (mid May to early November), cormorants, Brant, Surf and White-winged Scoters, up to 10 species of gulls, and terns. If there is a rip-tide off the end of the spit, this can be a good place to view Marbled Murrelet. Sometimes in fall, Parasitic Jaeger can be seen chasing Common Tern. Walking the beach to the right (south) may produce both golden-plovers, and sometimes Baird's or Buff-breasted Sandpipers. Gray Whales are occasionally seen from this location between March and May and even during some summers.. On the south side of Damon Point, near the east end, 2 Long-billed Murrelets were observed in early August 1999.

The beach grass along both sides of Damon Point Road may contain Horned Lark (resident), American Pipit (spring and fall), Palm Warbler (rare, in Scotch Broom in fall and winter), Savannah Sparrow, Lapland Longspur (fall), Snow Bunting (winter), and Western Meadowlark. Winter rarities at Damon Point have included Gyrfalcon, Snowy Owl, American Tree Sparrow, and even McKay's Bunting.

The **Ocean Shores Marina** is located along Marine View Drive, near the base of Damon Point. Here birders can watch, often at very close range, Red-throated, Pacific, Common, and very rarely Yellow-billed (three records) Loons, Horned, Eared, and Clark's Grebes (latter two, rare in winter), Double-crested, Brandt's and Pelagic Cormorants, gulls, and Belted Kingfisher. Birds may seek protection from winter storms in the marina. Watch for Purple Martin in late spring to late summer.

Explore the Scotch Broom between the Marina and Discovery Avenue, and on either side of Point Brown Avenue where it intersects with Discovery Avenue, for Spotted Towhee and White-crowned and Golden-crowned (winter) Sparrows. The intersection of Discovery Avenue and Point Brown Avenue is one of the most reliable spots in the state for Palm Warbler (fall and winter). Tropical Kingbird has been recorded in this general area from mid October to late November. Also, search for Palm Warbler in the Scotch Broom and short pines between the marina and the Harbor Pointe Shores retirement facility along Catala Avenue.

A passenger-only ferry links Ocean Shores to Westport during the summer months and leaves from the marina. Occasionally, Gray Whales summer in the waters off the tip of Damon Point and the ferry may detour to get closer views of these magnificent mammals.

Located north of the **Ocean Shores Environmental Interpretive Center** (at the junction of Discovery Avenue and Catala Avenue) is a small patch of spruce woods that may hold a good variety of birds and occasional migrants. The trees are north of the marina and northeast of the Discovery Inn. Explore the woods and surrounding brush for Hutton's Vireo, Black-capped and Chestnut-backed Chickadees, Bushtit, Red-breasted Nuthatch, Bewick's and Winter Wrens, Black-throated Gray (May through September) and Townsend's Warblers. A Blackburnian Warbler was seen here in September 1979. A bird-sighting log is located outside the front door of the Interpretive Center. Check for the latest local birding reports. Take the time to examine the coastal wildlife exhibits at the Interpretive Center. Also, check the freshwater canal near the inn. American Bittern and Green Heron are sometimes seen amidst the cattails.

The **Inner Bay** along the eastern edge of Ocean Shores can be great birding for geese, ducks, curlews, godwits, small sandpipers, and gulls - especially one to two hours before or after high tide. The best viewing spot is the **Wildlife Viewing Lot** on North Bay Avenue, which gives good views of the inner bay and access to **Bill's Spit**, a sand spit directly offshore. Nearby Peninsula Court cul-de-sac, also provides access to the beach

Bill's Spit   Bob Morse

through a poorly marked public easement. Once on the beach, walk left (north) to Bill's Spit with its roosting geese, ducks, Willet (rare), Whimbrel, Long-billed Curlew, Hudsonian (September 1992) and Bar-tailed Godwits (rare in fall), Marbled Godwit, and a host of other shorebirds, a myriad of gulls, and in October 1999 an Eurasian Dotterel and American Avocet. Bill's Spit and Tokeland are probably the two most reliable spots in the lower 48 states for Bar-tailed Godwit in the fall. Please avoid flushing birds resting on the spit. Brant can sometimes be seen out in the bay and at low tide Harbor Seals haul out on the sandbars.

Good woodlot birding is available along Wakina Loop from Peninsula Court to Alpine Court in the mixed coniferous and broadleaf woods.

The Ocean Shores Fire Station is located on the east side of Pt. Brown Avenue, just south of McDonald's in downtown Ocean Shores. A small, freshwater biofiltration wetland, a.k.a. **Fire Station Pond**, exists just south of the fire station across K Lewis Road. A good variety of shorebirds have appeared in this small pond, including a Stilt Sandpiper in June 1998. Two Redheads put in an appearance in October 1999.

Students at the North Beach Middle and Senior High School, with partial funding by the Quinault Indian Nation, have built a 1¼ mile trail around **Cyber Lake**, just north of the Ocean Shores city limits. The small, freshwater lake is located on the west and north side of SR 115, near the school.

Park in the school parking lot, walk across the field to a trailhead located at the southwest corner of the lake (a Public Trail sign may be visible from SR 115). The trail may be slippery in places as it goes around the shallow lake. A shelter on an overlook on the northwest side gives a good view down the lake. Beyond the shelter, the trail crosses a footbridge where close studies of roosting shorebirds is possible during migration.

Water birds include Pied-billed Grebe, Great Blue and Green Herons, Trumpeter Swan, Wood Duck (summer), and Lesser Scaup. When the water level is low, check for dowitchers. During migration, good numbers of Greater Yellowlegs with the occasional Lesser Yellowlegs often roost at the south end of the lake.

The surrounding coniferous and broadleaf woods host Anna's Hummingbird (rare in winter), Hairy Woodpecker, occasional Olive-sided Flycatcher (summer), Hutton's Vireo, Black-capped and Chestnut-backed Chickadees, Bewick's Wren, Cedar Waxwing, Purple and House Finches, Red Crossbill, and American Goldfinch. Check for warblers and vireos in migration.

The **airport** along Olympic Avenue and Duck Lake Drive sometimes has large flocks of Canada Geese. A Mountain Bluebird was seen here in May 2001. (The airport is open to the public but watch for incoming planes.)

Drive north of the airport to **Fathom Street**, for views of flocks of geese, ducks, and shorebirds in the bay.

Any of the trees in the airport area may have Northern Shrike or any number of raptors. A Bald Eagle regularly hunts this area. To the south of the airport and opposite 223 Olympic View Avenue, there is an obscure path that leads across an open field toward the bay. A narrow boardwalk crosses a marsh where Virginia Rail may be heard, especially early in the morning.

There are a number of excellent points on **Duck Lake** to view a vast array of grebes, geese, ducks, or bathing gulls including the two viewing areas where Overlake Street crosses Duck Lake. **Chinook Park**, just off Duck Lake Drive, provides good views of the lake, and has picnic tables, a restroom, and a small dock.

The **Weatherwax** property has been purchased by the City of Ocean Shores and its future use is currently under study. To access this large tract of land, walk the dirt/sand road that starts between the Elks Club and the PUD substation at the junction of Ocean Lake Way and Dolphin Avenue. The road travels south and parallels a powerline through a $1/2$ mile of mixed coniferous and broadleaf woods to eventually end at Draconia Avenue. This area has been good for Hutton's Vireo, Yellow-rumped, Black-throated Gray, and Townsend's Warblers, Purple and House Finches, and Red Crossbill.

Burrows Road
(See Moclips to Ocean City map)

From Ocean Shores take SR 115 and SR 109 toward Hoquiam. This section of SR 109 is a corridor cut through the large tracts of Douglas fir that are common along the coast. About three miles beyond Hogan's Corner (the intersection of SR 115 and SR 109) the **Burrows Road** leads off to the right. This loop road offers a few opportunities to scan the salt marshes and the North Bay for waterfowl and wintering raptors.

Grays Harbor National Wildlife Refuge

At MP 1.5, just before entering Hoquiam, take a right onto Paulson Road at the **Grays Harbor National Wildlife Refuge** sign. A Swamp Sparrow was located in the cattail marsh on the right in February 1998. At the "T" junction, go right on Airport Way past the sewage lagoon and park across from Lana's Cafe. To get to the best viewing areas, walk around the gate, go west along the airport pavement, and then take the ¾ mile **Sandpiper Trail** to the shorebird viewing areas.

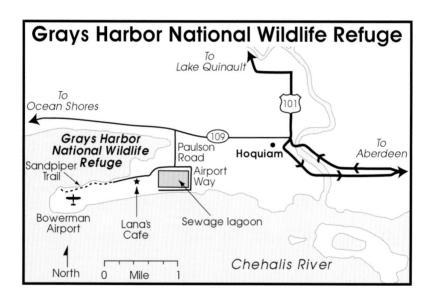

Grays Harbor National Wildlife Refuge

During spring migration the Grays Harbor National Wildlife Refuge (a.k.a. **Bowerman Basin**) with its 1,500 acres of salt marshes and mudflats is a fantastic place to study shorebirds.

It may be difficult to fully appreciate the importance of this wildlife refuge to the migration of hundreds of thousands of shorebirds that stop here to feed and rest before continuing on their 7,000 mile journey from South America to their nesting grounds in the arctic. The Grays Harbor estuary is one of eight sites in North America to be designated a Western Hemisphere

Shorebird Reserve Network Site of hemispheric importance. This is because of the high concentration of amphipods in these mudflats (up to 55,000 per cubic meter) which provide a rich food supply for the migrating shorebirds.

Grays Harbor NWR   Stuart MacKay/ USF&WS

The peak of spring migration occurs during the last week of April and the first week in May. The annual Grays Harbor Shorebird Festival is held during this time to coincide with the peak of migration. The best time to view the shorebirds is an hour or two before and after high tide when the shorebirds feed in the mud close to shore. At this time, there can be tens of thousands of shorebirds available for close, detailed study. Conversely, when the tide is out, few shorebirds remain as they feed on other parts of the Grays Harbor estuary.

The most prevalent spring shorebirds are Western Sandpiper, Dunlin, and Short-billed Dowitcher. Others to search for include Black-bellied and Semipalmated Plovers, Greater Yellowlegs, Red Knot, and Least Sandpiper. Merlin and Peregrine Falcon regularly hunt here and provide a fascinating sight as the "flying balls" of shorebirds maneuver to avoid these predators. Check for Peregrine Falcon perched on tall structures (navigational towers, light standards at the dock, telephone poles, and pilings).

Flocks of migrating shorebirds and waterfowl (watch for Greater White-fronted Goose and Eurasian Wigeon) are present in smaller numbers in fall. Large flocks of Dunlin may be found on the mudflats in winter. American White Pelican, Snowy Egret, Snow and Ross's Geese, and Sandhill Crane have put in appearances in the saltwater marsh here.

Sandpiper Trail   Art Pavey/USF&WS

On the way out, check the north side of the **sewage lagoon** for grebes (Eared, rare in winter), Cinnamon Teal (early to mid spring), phalaropes (Red-necked, during fall migration and Red, after winter storms), gulls (Franklin, rare in migration), and other waterfowl. A Tufted Duck was seen in the sewage lagoon in March 2000 and again in 2001. Follow Airport Way around to the south side of the lagoon. The Chehalis River mudflats host ducks, shorebirds, gulls, and terns. Walk the grassy areas just to the south of the sewage lagoon for sparrows and the occasional Lapland and Chestnut-collared Longspur (latter, one record) in fall. Palm Warblers have been seen here as well.

Return to SR 109, go through Hoquiam (the road becomes US 101) and follow US 101 south through Aberdeen.

Aberdeen

The **Lake Swano Nature Trails**, at the Grays Harbor Community College, provide easy access to good birding close to downtown Aberdeen. The gravel trails loop through stands of broadleaf and coniferous woods with nearby shrubby thickets. The model watershed project here is designed to improve the local salmon stream and rearing habitats.

A variety of birds here include Bewick's and Winter Wrens, Hermit and Varied (winter) Thrushes, Black-throated Gray Warbler, and Western Tanager (summer).

From downtown Aberdeen, travel south on US 101 and cross the bridge over the Chehalis River. Stay in the right lane and continue straight onto State Route 105. Proceed 0.6 miles along SR 105 and turn left at Edward P. Smith Drive, the entrance to the Grays Harbor Community College. Continue 0.1 mile to where the road splits. Veer left into the parking lot. The trailhead and map is at the east end of the parking lot near the Aquaculture Center.

Two trails depart from the bridge near here. The Poggie Trail (to the left, before the bridge) follows Alder Creek for 0.5 miles passing through alder stands with nearby salmonberry and red elderberry. In winter, look for "Sooty" Fox and Golden-crowned Sparrows. In spring watch for migrating warblers and in summer look for Rufous Hummingbirds.

The second trail is the Forest Trail, 0.3 miles long, which enters the mixed coniferous woods after the bridge (stay right at the fork and follow the numbered markers). Look for Black-capped and Chestnut-backed Chickadees, Brown Creeper, Winter Wren, Golden-crowned Kinglet, and Varied Thrush. There are large excavations in some trees, indicating Pileated Woodpeckers. The trail then becomes the Alder Creek Trail as it parallels Alder Creek to return in a short distance to the bridge.

Two more trails can be accessed from the parking lot at the Diesel Mechanics Building. To get there, follow the unmarked road just above the lower parking lot. Maps are posted near the parking areas. The Nice Creek Trail is almost a half mile long and connects to the ³/₄ mile Lake Swano Trail. Look for Pied-billed Grebe, Mallard, Hooded Merganser, and possibly Wood Duck on the lake.

Lake Swano/Friends Landing

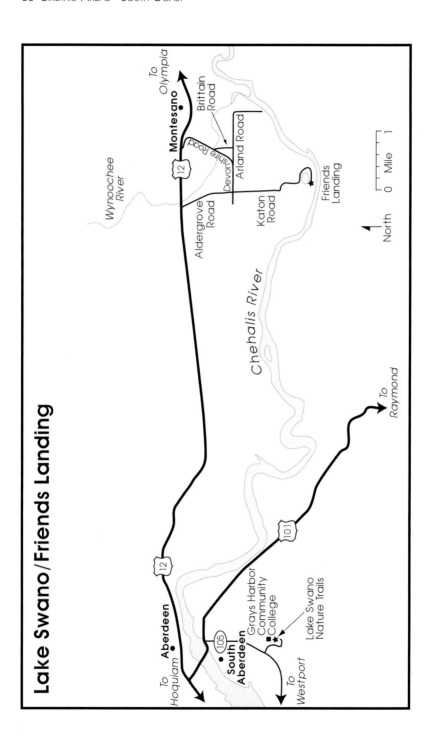

Friends Landing

For a side trip to the better birding spots east of Aberdeen, go east from Aberdeen on US 12 about eight miles to its intersection with Aldergrove Road. Just before the Wynoochee River bridge, turn right onto Aldergrove Road, heading south. At 0.9 miles cross the railroad tracks and the Devonshire Road and continue straight onto Katon Road. Check the fields for Savannah Sparrow and blackbirds and the trees and shrubs for the occasional Western Scrub-Jay. American Kestrel hunt from the wires along the road. Check for Belted Kingfisher at the bridge. Continue to the **Friends Landing** boat launch area. RV and tent camping is available here in summer. Search the waters of the Chehalis River for Hooded and Common Mergansers.

The boardwalk and path around the small freshwater lake goes through a chaotic tangle of alder, ferns, and firs typical of riparian flood plains. "Flood" is an active verb along the Chehalis River so beware of water across the entry road or path. Birds of the thickets include Black-capped and Chestnut-backed Chickadees, Bewick's Wren, Hermit Thrush (winter), American Robin, Spotted Towhee, "Sooty" Fox (winter), Song, White-crowned, and Golden-crowned (winter) Sparrows, and Dark-eyed Junco. Look for Red-breasted Sapsucker, Downy Woodpecker, Willow Flycatcher (summer), Ruby-crowned Kinglet (winter), and Cedar Waxwing in nearby trees. Bald Eagle may have a nest in the evergreen trees to the west or south of the lake. Double-crested Cormorant and Pied-billed Grebe frequent the river and the lake. In the lake edges, check for Great Blue Heron, Marsh Wren, and Common Yellowthroat (summer).

When returning, turn right on Devonshire Road and go 0.4 miles to where the Devonshire Road veers left. Go straight onto **Arland Road** and follow the road to its end. Check the large barn on the left (at the corner) for Band-tailed Pigeon and Western Scrub-Jay. In winter, flooded field ponds along the road may have Northern Shoveler, Northern Pintail, Canvasback, Ruddy Duck, as well as other ducks. There is a swampy area 1/2 mile past the barn on the right that has had Virginia Rails. On the left, look for

Black-throated Gray Warbler in the alder and maple trees in summer. When returning, turn right at Brittain Road and check the thickets for Spotted Towhee, White-throated Sparrow (rare in winter), White-crowned, and Golden-crowned (winter) Sparrows. At the Devonshire Road, turn right and proceed 0.4 miles back to US 12.

Monte Brady Loop Road

This 7 mile loop travels through open farmlands and is best after rains have created shallow ponds which attract good numbers of wintering waterfowl. The fields during migration, especially when flooded, can be good for shorebirds including golden-plovers. A variety of raptors regularly hunt these fields in winter including Bald Eagle, Northern Harrier, Cooper's, Red-shouldered (one record), Red-tailed, Rough-legged Hawks, American Kestrel, Merlin, Peregrine Falcon, Gyrfalcon (rare), and Short-eared Owl. Barn and Great-horned Owls also have been recorded.

Travel east from Aberdeen on US 12 and at MP 12.5 turn right onto the Monte Brady Road. Start all mileages from here. At 0.9 miles, turn right onto the Brady Loop Road.

In winter, the field ponds along the **Brady Loop Road** may have Trumpeter and Tundra Swans, Eurasian and American

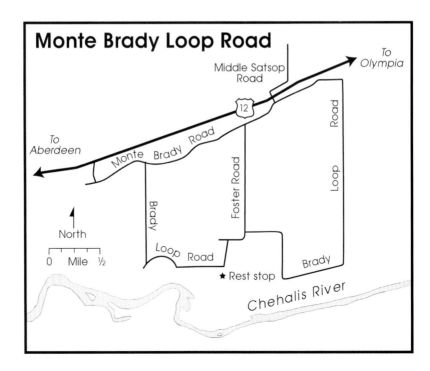

Wigeons, Mallard, Northern Shoveler, Northern Pintail, Green-winged Teal, Bufflehead, and American Coot. The nearby open fields have flocks of wintering Canada Geese. Many of the fields along this loop route are regulated hunting areas. Some parts of the Brady Loop Road are subject to flooding in winter if the nearby Chehalis River overflows its banks. Beware of any water over the road.

Check the weeds, fence lines, and shrubby thickets along the road for sparrows, Spotted Towhee, and warblers in season. In winter, Merlin, Peregrine Falcon, Short-eared Owl, or even a Gyrfalcon may be hunting these fields. At 1.9 miles, the road takes a left turn and the stand of red alders and shrubby thickets (on the right between the road and the river) should be checked for Downy Woodpecker, flycatchers, chickadees, Bewick's Wren, Ruby-crowned Kinglet (winter), warblers (in season), "Sooty" Fox (winter), Song, and White-throated (rare) Sparrows.

At 2.6 miles there is rest stop and access to the Chehalis River. Ring-necked Pheasant may be in the area.

At 3.2 miles the Brady Loop Road turns right while the Foster Road continues straight ahead to meet the Monte Brady Road in a mile further. This section of the Foster Road has hosted Cooper's Hawk, wintering Rough-legged Hawk, Peregrine Falcon, Black-bellied Plover, Killdeer, Dunlin, Common Snipe (in wetter, grassy areas), and Western Meadowlark.

Return to the Brady Loop Road and continue along this road. Scan the ponds along the road for ducks. Alder trees around the ponds may have Red-tailed Hawk, Bald Eagle, or other raptors. Swans may be either in the larger ponds or open fields. Western Scrub-Jay should be searched for around farmhouses. This area has only recently been heavily birded and continues to yield surprises. Whimbrel and several Sandhill Crane were noted in spring 2001.

At 7.1 miles, turn right at the Monte Brady Road and, in a few hundred feet, return to US 12.

Mt. Quail have been seen in the past in limited numbers in

the clear cuts and short vegetation along the Middle Satsop Road north of Brady. To reach this area, cross over US 12, following the Monte Brady Road. At the stop sign take an odometer reading and proceed straight ahead onto the Middle Satsop Road. At 4 miles check the gravel pit on the left. Just after crossing into Mason County at 8 miles, turn right at the Schafer Park Road and check the old clear cuts in this area. Suitable habitat for Mt. Quail exists in old clear cuts with Scotch Broom, salal, and other short vegetation.

Or, continue north on the Middle Satsop Road and veer left onto West Boundary Road. Check the habitat on the right for the next 1.2 miles, then turn right on the West Boundary Cutoff road to return to the Middle Satsop Road.

There are a number of old logging roads crossing these clear cuts that can be walked to look and listen for Mt. Quail. The best time is at dawn in spring when they are calling.

More recent sightings of Mt. Quail have been along the Cloquallum Road northeast of Elma.

Vance Creek Park, Wenzel Slough, Keys Road Loop

This 10 mile loop is best in winter and early spring when the fields are flooded. The loop starts at the intersection of US 12 and Keys Road, just east of the Satsop River bridge, about 16 miles east of Aberdeen.

Travel east on US 12 and turn right onto **Schouweiler Road**, just past MP 18. Turn left at the stop sign following the road to its end in front of a metal gate. Park* out of the way and proceed, on foot, around the gate, into the Washington Department of Fish and Wildlife's 527 acre Chehalis Wildlife Area with its freshwater ponds, surrounded by shrubby thickets, and stands of broadleaf woods. Parts of the wildlife area may be flooded from winter rains. The birding in the adjacent fields and thickets usually produces a good mixture of sparrows, with geese and ducks in the sloughs and ponds, and raptors hunting the fields. American Bittern, Virginia Rail, Marsh Wren, or Common Yellowthroat

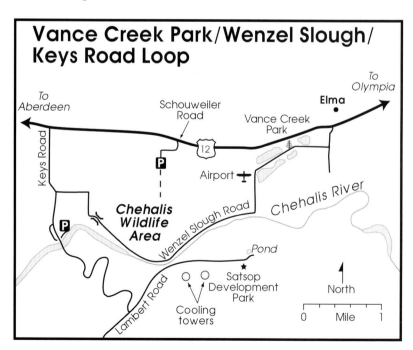

(summer) may call from the freshwater marshes. Explore the trails from the parking area to check the ponds, shrubby thickets, and stands of broadleaf woods.

* A Washington Department of Fish and Wildlife Access Stewardship Decal is needed to park here. Details on obtaining a decal are provided in the More Coastal Information Appendix.

Return to US 12 and continue right (east). Take the 3rd Street, Elma exit and turn right at the stop sign. In ¼ mile, turn right at the Vance Creek Park and airport signs onto Wenzel Slough Road.

A small parking lot for **Vance Creek Park** is on the right and the pond should be checked for Pied-billed Grebe, Canada Goose, Ring-necked Duck, scaup, Bufflehead, American Coot, and bathing gulls. The pond can have a good number of waterfowl in winter. Check the snags to the south for an Osprey nest.

Continue west on **Wenzel Slough Road** and pull into the main parking lot. A Yellow-billed Cuckoo was seen to the west of the footbridge in August 1996. Check the long pond to the west of the parking lot for grebes and Double-crested Cormorant and take the path along Vance Creek (between the long pond and the highway) and watch for thrushes and sparrows especially during migration.

Continue west on the Wenzel Slough Road. Check the half hidden ponds on the south side of the road for swans, ducks, cormorants, and grebes. Check the airport fields for plovers, Killdeer, and migrating yellowlegs.

Continue on the Wenzel Slough Road, which parallels the Chehalis River. In winter, the Chehalis River may overflow its banks and flood the road. It is advisable to not drive through any standing water on the road; it may be deeper than it appears. Over the next 3 miles, the open fields on the right can have large or small ponds in winter depending on the amount of rain. The variety of ducks includes Eurasian and American Wigeons, Mallard, Northern Pintail, Green-winged Teal, Ring-necked Duck, Bufflehead, and even a Garganey (spring of 1991). During hunting season, the ducks in these ponds are skittish and the use of the car as a blind may allow the best view. Do not enter the fields without permission.

Swans may winter in the flooded fields on the right while, further along, shorebirds and gulls occupy the shallow, wet fields to the left of the road. Check the thickets beside the road for Dark-eyed Junco and a mixture of sparrows. Pause at the small bridge to search for wintering ducks in the creek and fields.

Just after the bridge, the road makes a right turn. A small pond on the left, just before the road turns left, can have occasional ducks, yellowlegs, or plovers after winter rains. A Sandhill Crane was seen here in the spring of 1999. Mew Gull may be in adjacent fields in winter. On the right, the flooded fields in winter have ducks and gulls. Keep a watch for Bald Eagle, Northern Harrier, Red-tailed Hawk, and a number of other raptors anywhere along this road.

At the intersection of the Wenzel Slough Road and the Keys Road, the birder can take an additional 9 mile side trip to the **Satsop Development Park**. To do so, turn left and proceed about 3 miles to the Lambert Road. Turn left and go 1.5 miles past the massive cooling towers, to a fenced pond inside a Wildlife Mitigation Area on the left. In winter, this pond may hold a staggering number of ducks for its size. Here seeking refuge from local hunters, the more common ducks are both wigeons, Mallard, Northern Pintail, Ring-necked Duck, and American Coot.

Return to the Keys Road. Just after the bridge, turn left and follow the paved road to a Washington Department of Fish Wildlife parking area* at the end. Explore the shrubby thickets adjoining the Chehalis River for "Sooty" Fox and Golden-crowned Sparrows (winter). Return on the Keys Road to US 12.

* A Washington Department of Fish and Wildlife Access Stewardship Decal is required to park here.

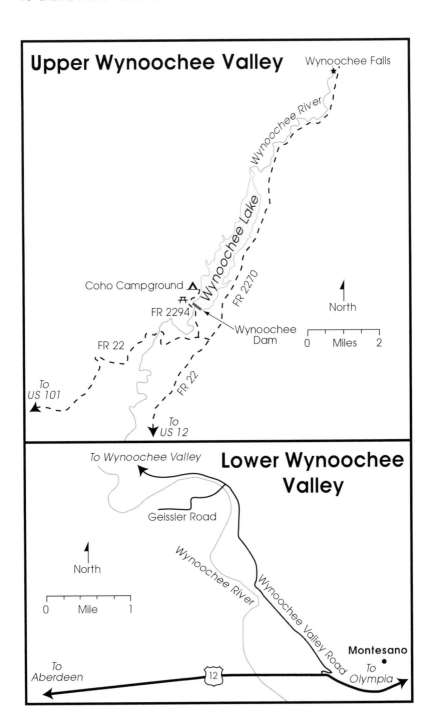

Upper Wynoochee Valley

Wynoochee Falls

Wynoochee River

Wynoochee Lake

Coho Campground

FR 2294

FR 2270

Wynoochee Dam

North

0 Miles 2

FR 22

To US 101

FR 22

To US 12

Lower Wynoochee Valley

To Wynoochee Valley

Geissler Road

Wynoochee River

Wynoochee Valley Road

North

0 Mile 1

Montesano

To Olympia

To Aberdeen

12

Wynoochee Valley

The Wynoochee Valley extends north 35 miles along the Wynoochee River from Montesano through farmlands and managed forests of Douglas fir, western red cedar, and western hemlock to Wynoochee Lake and Wynoochee Falls. Wynoochee Lake is 12 miles east of Lake Quinault and 15 miles west of Lake Cushman and just below the southern border of the Olympic National Park. The upper part of the Wynoochee Valley Road allows access to some of the higher elevations birds.

Just west of Montesano on US 12, at MP 11.5, take the Devonshire Road exit. At the north side of the freeway, go left onto the **Wynoochee Valley Road**. The first part of this road travels by open farmlands surrounded by broadleaf trees and shrubby thickets. There are a number of places to stop and bird along the road although pullouts are limited. **Geissler Road** (on the left at 2.8 miles) as well as the Public Fishing area (a little further north) are good places to stop to check the river, bordering trees, and shrubby thickets for passerines and wintering sparrows. Continuing along the Wynoochee Valley Road, scan the freshwater marshes and ponds for Great Blue Heron, Common Snipe and ducks.

Gradually, the valley narrows and open farmlands give way to hillsides of managed forests of Douglas fir, western red cedar, and western hemlock. At about 18 miles, the road becomes dirt as it enters the Olympic National Forest. Now FR 22, the road continues through stands of coniferous woods and occasional clear cuts. From here north, check for Warbling Vireo (along streams), and Purple Finch and Red Crossbill in the conifers.

Pass by the site of Camp Grisdale, a logging camp that flourished here from 1946 until 1985. There is still a significant amount of timber harvesting occurring in these woods and logging trucks pass by at harrowing speeds.

At 35 miles, FR 22 goes left. Continue straight ahead on FR 2270 for another nine miles to **Wynoochee Falls**. After a few miles the road, which runs along the east side of Wynoochee Lake, is blocked by a gate from October 1 through April 30. In early summer, along this road, and at the north end near Wynoochee Falls, birds of the higher elevation may be heard or seen. Look and listen for Blue Grouse (calling in early May), passing Band-tailed Pigeons, Western Screech-Owl, Hammond's and Pacific-slope Flycatchers, Warbling Vireo, Swainson's Thrush (wetter areas), Hermit Thrush (forest edges), Varied Thrush, and Western Tanager.

Return south to FR 22 and turn right. In ¼ miles, turn right on FR 2294 toward Wynoochee Dam. After passing the outflow of the dam, turn right to the Visitor Center, restrooms, and an overlook of the river below.

Continue north on FR 2294 and turn right at the **Wynoochee Lake Dam and Picnic Area** sign. This day use site offers swimming, picnic tables, lush coniferous forests, and scenic views of Wynoochee Lake and neighboring mountains.

Continue north on FR 2294 and turn right into the USFS **Coho Campground** (open in summer). Search for Northern Pygmy-Owl, Vaux's Swift, Pileated Woodpecker, Gray Jay, White-crowned Sparrow, and Black-headed Grosbeak.

From the campground return to Montesano via FR 22 and the Wynoochee Valley Road or go west on FR 22 and then Donkey Creek Road about 22 miles to get to US 101 near Humptulips.

Along FR 22 heading west, in summer, search for Olive-sided and Willow Flycatchers, Black-throated Gray and Wilson's Warblers.

Johns River Wildlife Area

In Aberdeen, follow US 101 through town and then across the Chehalis River bridge. After the bridge, the highway splits with US 101 going left and SR 105 proceeding straight ahead. Take SR 105 towards Westport.

About 13 miles from Aberdeen, just after the Johns River, turn left onto Johns River Road. Bear left at the "Y" with the "Welcome to John's River" sign, then left at the stop sign. Bear right down the hill to the Washington Department of Fish and Wildlife **Johns River Wildlife Area**. A Washington Department of Fish and a Wildlife Access Stewardship Decal.is required to park here. Information on obtaining a decal is provided in the More Coastal Information Appendix.

Johns River Wildlife Area   Bob Morse

The 1500 acre wildlife area here consists of open farmlands and freshwater and salt water marshes. A dike parallels the Johns River with a tidal salt water marsh on the river side of the dike and open fields and freshwater sloughs and marshes on the inside. The dike trail is paved for the first ½ mile ending at a photo blind where studies of the fields should produce Canada

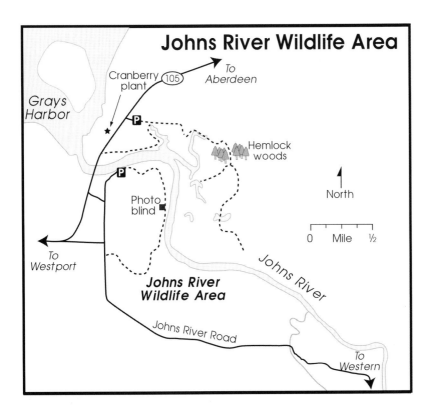

Johns River Wildlife Area

Goose, ducks, Northern Harrier, Red-tailed Hawk, and occasionally, Short-eared Owl and Roosevelt Elk. In the wetter areas, Virginia Rail and Common Snipe have been seen.

To sample the owling in this general area, return to the "Welcome to John's River" sign and proceed south 3.4 miles along Johns River Road to **Western**, a collection of farms near the Johns River. Predawn owling along the road with adjoining broadleaf woods has produced Western Screech, Great Horned, and Barred (one record) Owls. Northern Saw-whet Owls have been heard calling in predawn hours in the coniferous woods between Western and SR 105.

The habitat on the east side of the Johns River Wildlife Area is different with coniferous forests of western hemlock, western red cedar, and Sitka spruce and broadleaf woods dominated by red alder. To reach this area, return to SR 015 and turn right (east). Cross the Johns River bridge and, in about ¹/₂ mile, turn right into a parking area. Proceed on foot past the metal gate on a road which travels by broadleaf woods and shrubby thickets with the diked freshwater marsh on the right. The road crosses two salt water marshes (check for Wood Duck at the second marsh in spring and summer), climbs into a short section of conifers and then starts down a short hill toward the marsh. At this point, about ¹/₄ mile from the parking area, a dike trail leads off to the right. This dike trail reaches the river and then parallels the river all the way back to SR 105 to emerge just east of the Johns River bridge. In winter, the lands inside the dike are flooded and Canada Goose, ducks, and occasional Common Snipe are seen with Red-tailed Hawk patrolling overhead. Among the dike trail blackberry bushes expect to find Golden-crowned Sparrows in winter.

If, instead of taking this dike trail, the birder were to continue along the road, stands of conifers are encountered where Hutton's Vireo may respond to "pishing" along with Golden-crowned Kinglet and Chestnut-backed Chickadee. After climbing a small hill, a picturesque, moss draped hemlock forest is soon reached. Here, 10 foot diameter stumps remind us of the giant trees that once dominated this landscape. The woods host Ruffed and Blue Grouse, Band-tailed Pigeon (spring through fall), Northern Flicker, both chickadees, Bewick's and Winter Wrens, both kinglets, Yellow-rumped Warbler, Spotted Towhee, and Dark-eyed Junco. Eventually the road splits and both parts of the road end at salt water marshes where the dikes have been breached.

Bottle Beach State Park

Continue west on SR 105 to MP 34.7 and turn right onto a short gravel road (opposite Ocosta Third Street). This is the entrance to the undeveloped Bottle Beach State Park. Park on the gravel road before the barricade.

This place has an interesting history. The site at Bottle Beach was platted as the town of Ocosta in 1889 when the Northern Pacific Railroad designated Ocosta as their Pacific terminus for all goods being shipped to Portland, San Francisco, and the Orient. Ocosta quickly grew, reaching a population of 450 by 1892. Steamers and sailing ships tied up to the 2,900 foot long dock that stretched into the bay. Within three years the town had over 30 businesses including a post office, several real estate companies, a glass factory, mills, saloons, a brewing company, and a newspaper.

In 1893, after long debate, the railroad decided to change its terminus to Tacoma and stopped using Ocosta as a shipping port. Ocosta's population and businesses slowly declined so that today all of Ocosta has disappeared except for one Victorian residence (still visible on Ocosta Myrtle Street), pilings from the old dock, and the brick foundation of a railroad engine turnaround (still visible on the beach). Parts of the railroad trestle and railroad bed also appear along the beach. The town has reverted to pasture land now grazed by horses and cows.

Through the efforts of birders Ruby Egbert and Bob Morse, this property was acquired by Washington State Parks in 1993 and designated as **Bottle Beach State Park** and Ruby Egbert Natural Area.

The undeveloped state park is open to birders but there is limited parking in front of the road barricade. Walk around the barricade, cross a small bridge, and follow the path to the beach. Shorebird viewing can be quite good on the mudflats during spring migration, especially an hour and a half before and after high tide. Bottle Beach is one of the best places to watch shorebirds in the Grays Harbor estuary because its mudflats are one of the last to be covered by the incoming tide. It is a good place to see Red Knot in spring. Fall shorebirds found here include Black-bellied, Pacific and American Golden-Plovers, Semipalmated Plovers, Whimbrel, Marbled Godwit, and Short-billed and Long-billed Dowitchers.

This 70 acre state park, when developed, will include a parking area, kiosk, viewing platforms, and a trail through the nearby spruce woods.

Over 130 species of birds have already been recorded. The best places to bird are along the beach and the spruce woods at the east edge of the property. A Blue-gray Gnatcatcher was seen near the road barricade in February 1983. The willow thickets should be checked for migrant passerines and the nearby freshwater marshes for Virginia Rail and migrating Lincoln's Sparrow.

Continue west on SR 105. Just west of the Elk River bridge is **Brady's Oysters**, a retail outlet, well known for its fresh oysters and seafood. From Brady's, scan the Elk River for loons, grebes, ducks and, if the tide is out, shorebirds. A public restroom is available here. Northern Saw-whet Owls may be calling from conifers to the west in the pre-dawn hours.

Continue west on SR 105.

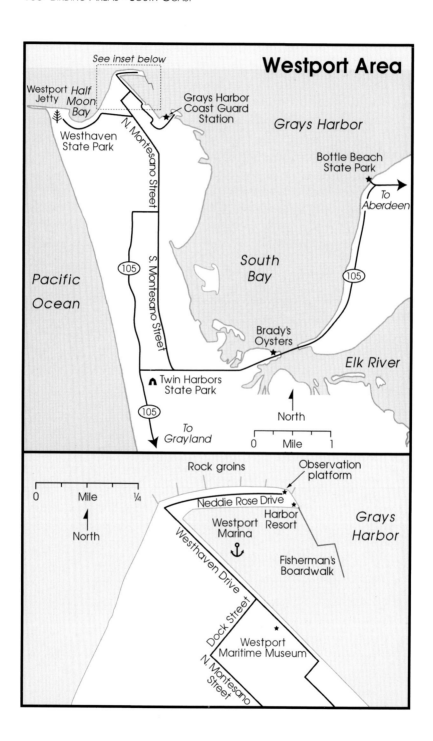

Westport Area

See inset below

Westport Jetty

Half Moon Bay

Westhaven State Park

Grays Harbor Coast Guard Station

Grays Harbor

N. Montesano Street

Bottle Beach State Park

To Aberdeen

105

S. Montesano Street

Pacific Ocean

105

South Bay

Brady's Oysters

105

Elk River

Twin Harbors State Park

North

To Grayland

0   Mile   1

Rock groins

Observation platform

Mile   ¼

Neddie Rose Drive

Harbor Resort

Grays Harbor

North

Westport Marina

Westhaven Drive

Fisherman's Boardwalk

Dock Street

N. Montesano Street

Westport Maritime Museum

Westport

Westport is a good place to check for Great Egret in winter. The two best spots are the very western edge of the salt water marsh north of SR 105 at MP 31 and in the fields to the east of Bayside Plaza (509 S. Montesano Street - the main road coming into Westport).

Follow the signs to Westport and the Westport Marina; observe posted speed limits. In December 1991, a Brambling was discovered in the blackberries where N. Montesano Street turns right and becomes Dock Street.

Westport Marina   Bob Morse

Where Dock Street intersects Westhaven Drive (the main street along the **Westport Marina**), turn left to the rock breakwater then right onto Neddie Rose Drive. Park at the end of the road and walk up onto the Westport Marina **observation platform** next to the public restroom. Gray Whales summer in the surrounding Grays Harbor channel. In season, scan for Red-throated, Pacific, and Common Loons, Red-necked and Western Grebes, three cormorant species, Surf and White-winged Scoters, and gulls. Parasitic Jaegers have been seen here chasing

Black-legged Kittiwake and Common Tern during migration. When strong winds blow in from the ocean, Black Turnstone, Surfbird, and Rock Sandpiper, normally on the jetties, may seek protection on the leeward side of the nearby **rock groins** to the west of the viewing platform.

Westport groins from Observation platform   Bob Morse

Nearby, a walkway next to the Harbor Resort leads down to the **Fisherman's Boardwalk** where families fish and crab in the boat basin. Walk along the docks to a pier at the end, which offers good views of grebes, cormorants, gulls, and terns. The pier pilings sometimes host Brown Pelican, Black Turnstone, and Surfbird. Check around the docks for Common and Yellow-billed (latter, rare in winter) Loons, Western Grebe, Long-tailed Duck, Barrow's Goldeneye, (latter two, uncommon fall through spring), Heermann's Gull (summer and fall), and Harbor Seal.

When returning on Neddie Rose Drive, in winter check the waters off the breakwater and rock groins for Western and Clark's Grebes (latter, rare), Common Murre, Pigeon Guillemot, and Marbled Murrelet.

Westport Fisherman's Boardwalk   Bob Morse

Black-legged Kittiwake can sometimes be seen in fall through spring perched on the pilings offshore from the Coast Guard Station boat ramp in Westport. Follow the road south along the docks past the Westport Maritime Museum to the Coast Guard Station.

Glaucous Gull is uncommon in Westport in winter, but a scan of gulls on the roofs of the seafood processing plants or nearby fields may produce one.

When leaving Westport, take the road west to Westhaven State Park (day use only) for access to the **Westport Jetty**. You can walk out on the rock jetty (difficult and treacherous) or from base of the jetty watch for Red-throated, Pacific, and Common Loons, Horned, Red-necked, and Western Grebes, Sooty (fall) and Short-tailed (rare, winter) Shearwaters, Surf and White-winged Scoters, Common Murre, Pigeon Guillemot, Marbled Murrelet, and Rhinoceros Auklet as they fly in and out of the harbor (especially at dawn). Some winters, Harlequin Ducks are just off the end of the jetty where it enters **Half Moon Bay**.

Westport is the "sports fishing capital of the world" and can be quite busy during the summer salmon, halibut, and albacore tuna season. Salmon fishing is also done in the boat basin as is

crabbing for Rock and Dungeness Crabs. Surf fishing for Sea
Perch occurs along the southern beaches and jetty fishing for Sea
Bass, Greenling, Perch, and   Ling Cod is common. Whale
watching trips both inside the harbor and on the ocean are
popular from early March through May. The waters near the
Westport Jetty are known to have the best surfing waves along
the Washington coast.

A passenger-only ferry links Westport to Ocean Shores with
a few trips a day during the summer months.

Westport Pelagic Trips

Westport is the starting point for day-long pelagic bird trips organized by **Westport Seabirds**.

Since the mid-1960s, boat trips from Westport have gone offshore to deep oceanic waters, looking for seabirds unlikely to be seen from shore. A number of species previously unknown for the state have been found on these trips and the trips have contributed much to our understanding of seabird status and distribution. Among pelagic bird trips in North America, Westport trips are known particularly for finding numbers of Black-footed Albatross, which have been seen on virtually every trip reaching outer continental shelf habitats, and Fork-tailed Storm-Petrel, seen on almost all trips between May and October.

Trips are run during all seasons, but most take place from spring into fall. Probable for the July to October period are Black-footed Albatross, Northern Fulmar, Pink-footed, Buller's (mid August to October) and Sooty Shearwaters, Fork-tailed Storm Petrel, Red-necked and Red Phalaropes, Pomarine, Parasitic and Long-tailed Jaegers (latter, August to early September), South Polar Skua, Black-legged Kittiwake, Sabine's Gull, Arctic Tern, Common Murre, Pigeon Guillemot, Marbled Murrelet, Cassin's and Rhinoceros Auklets and Tufted Puffin. Laysan Albatross, Flesh-footed Shearwater (best in October) and Leach's Storm-Petrel are possible. Xantus's Murrelet is present during some years, and Manx Shearwater occurred several times in the 1990s. Most trips go about 35 miles offshore to the edge of the continental shelf where seabirds congregate to take advantage of the upwelling. Other trips to oceanic waters 65-70 miles out, look for Pterodroma petrels like Mottled and Murphy's Petrels, and other intriguing possibilities. Commercial fishing boats attract certain seabirds and are checked when possible.

Winter and early spring trips are more dependent on weather than those during the summer and fall season. Though many species above are not present, this is the most likely season to see Laysan Albatross (most trips November to April), Short-tailed Shearwater, and Ancient Murrelet along with possibilities like

Short-tailed Albatross (seen twice), Shy Albatross (once), Red-legged Kittiwake, Thick-billed Murre, Parakeet Auklet, and Horned Puffin. On all trips rarities are possible and, needless to say, looked-for. Loons, cormorants, Brown Pelican, sea ducks, several species of gulls, Caspian and Common Terns, shorebirds, migrant land birds, fur seal, porpoise, whale, sea turtle, shark and other animals are also seen in season. Marine mammals are most likely in May and October, though this is quite variable. Each trip has a number of experts on board, eager to help locate and describe birds and other sea-life.

Beyond the animals, these trips offer an experience enjoyed by few travelers in our jet age - being out of sight of land, in the natural, moving, ocean environment, which readily demonstrates that the earth is indeed a sphere, and can show that the 'green flash' is real, to say nothing of discovering whether the birder is prone to mal de mer. Most trips leave about 6 a.m. and return about 4 p.m. and are aboard the Monte Carlo moored at Float 8.

Information on dates and details of trips can be obtained from Westport Seabirds, P. O. Box 665, Westport, WA 98595, (360-268-5222), via e-mail at pmand@techline.com or at their website at www.westportseabirds.com.

Birders will probably want to stay in Westport the night before the pelagic trip. Two motels that cater to birders are the McBee's Silver Sands Motel (1001 S. Montesano on the way into Westport), (360-268-9029), and the Albatross Motel (on Dock Street in downtown Westport), (360-268-9233).

After enjoying Westport, continue south on SR 105 toward Grayland, Tokeland, and Raymond.

Grayland

Twin Harbors State Park, along SR 105, with its 300 campsites, is the largest state park in the area. The campground and the ³/₄ mile trail leading through a narrow band of shore pine woods to the beach has produced mixed forest species such as resident Pileated Woodpecker and Hutton's Vireo. During spring migration, there can be flycatchers, vireos, warblers, and other passerines in the park.

Further south on SR 105, in **Grayland**, the Cranberry capital of Washington, there are a number of accommodations and beach accesses. At MP 25.7, just north of the Grays Harbor/Pacific county line, go right on **Cranberry Beach Road** to gain access to the beach. Grayland Beach State Park, nestled among broadleaf and pine forests with shrubby thickets, offers both tent camping and RV facilities.

At MP 23.9, go right (west) on **Midway Beach Road** to the beach. Recently, Snowy Plover have nested in the open dune grasses of the upper beach both north and south of the access road. Elegant Terns are rarely seen in summer along the Grayland beaches (typically during El Nino years).

South of Grayland, in North Cove, turn right at MP 22.3 onto the **Warrenton Cannery Road**. In winter, look for Snowy Plover feeding at the water's edge north and south of where the road meets the beach. If driving the beach here, be careful of getting stuck in the soft sand.

Further south along SR 105, from the North Cove Pioneer Cemetery to the Shoalwater Bay Indian Reservation, look for Bald Eagle perched in trees to the left of the road.

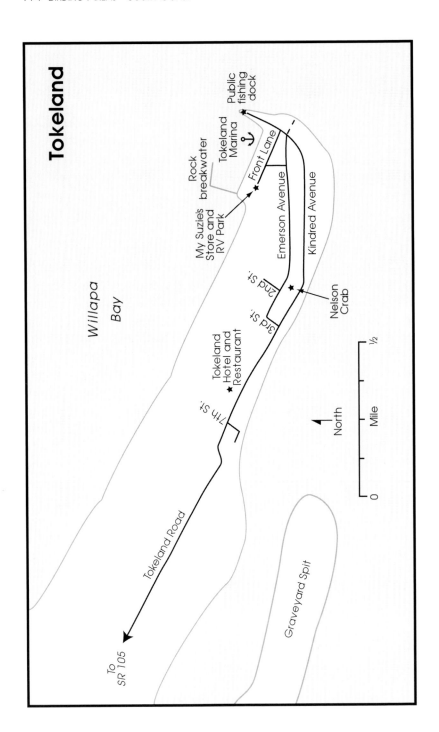

Tokeland

Willapa Bay

Public fishing dock

Tokeland Marina

Rock breakwater

Front Lane

Emerson Avenue

Kindred Avenue

My Suzies Store and RV Park

2nd St.

3rd St.

Nelson Crab

Tokeland Hotel and Restaurant

7th St.

North

Mile

0   ½

Tokeland Road

To SR 105

Graveyard Spit

Tokeland

Tokeland is known for its long-legged shorebirds such as Willet, Bar-tailed Godwit (rare in fall), Marbled Godwit, and Long-billed Curlew. It is also home to the Shoalwater Indians whose residence along this coast predates written history.

To get to Tokeland, follow the signs from SR 105 at the Shoalwater Bay Indian Reservation. Obey the 25 mph speed limit—it is strictly enforced.

Follow Tokeland Road and Kindred Avenue east towards Tokeland. Two miles from SR 105, turn right on 7th Street and park where the road makes a right turn (limited parking in front of rock wall). Walk out to the sandy beach and search the sand spit off shore (**Graveyard Spit**) and nearby beaches for Brown Pelican (spring through fall), Marbled Godwit, Long-billed Curlew, other shorebirds, and gulls. This is one of the most reliable spots in our state to find Willet and Long-billed Curlew in winter.

Continue east on Kindred Avenue to Tokeland. Stop at Nelson Crab, a retail outlet, for delicious fresh crab, shrimp, or smoked salmon (open daily 9:00 a.m. to 5:00 p.m.). The fields of Scotch Broom and Gorse east of Nelson Crab host Palm Warbler (rare, fall and winter), Spotted Towhee, Golden-Crowned Sparrow (winter), and American Goldfinch (summer).

Climb the rock wall across from these fields and scan the bay for loons, ducks, and gulls and the rocks and beach for Wandering Tattler and Ruddy and Black Turnstones.

Continue east on Kindred Avenue. Take a right at **Emerson Avenue** (hidden sign on left) and go a short distance to the end of the dirt road. Scan the beach, rocks, and pilings for cormorants. Willet, Whimbrel, Black Turnstone, Western, Herring (winter), and Glaucous-winged Gulls. A White-winged Dove was seen in this area in October 1999.

Return to Kindred Avenue, turn right and continue until the road ends at the **public fishing dock**. Park and check the bay for Common Loon, Western Grebe, Brown Pelican, Double-crested Cormorant, Brant (winter and spring), gulls, alcids (winter), or watch people tending their crab pots.

Tokeland Marina   Bob Morse

Check the **Tokeland Marina** on Front Lane and the long **rock breakwater** beyond the marina for flocks of large shorebirds. Up to 500 Marbled Godwits often congregate here at high tide and sometimes (mid August to mid October) a Bar-tailed Godwit or two is mixed in with the flock. In fall and winter, up to 15 Willets may be here at high tide. At low tide, the godwits can be anywhere in the Tokeland area, but have been most often seen on the beach at the marina, the mudflats to the west, the rock breakwater, Graveyard Spit by 7th Street, or near the North River mouth. Watch for Purple Martin in the marina (uncommon) from mid to late summer.

The area around the end of Tokeland is generally referred to as Toke Point.

Direct access to the rock breakwater and the surrounding salt water marsh can be obtained by driving west on Front Lane to **My Suzie's Store and RV Park**. Park out of the way and, if the store is open, ask the manager for permission to bird the area (they are birder friendly). Walk down the stairs at the west end of the RV park to gain access to the marsh and breakwater. The rock breakwater is one of the most reliable places to find Willet in the winter.

Tokeland breakwater   Bob Morse

In Tokeland, walk the small, dead end residential streets, e.g. 2nd Street, in search of fall vagrants such as Tropical Kingbird (early October to late November). Other rarities that have appeared in Tokeland include Clark's Grebe, Emperor Goose, American Avocet, Hudsonian Godwit, Elegant Tern, Northern Mockingbird, Lark Bunting, White-throated Sparrow, Chestnut-collared Longspur, and Hooded Oriole.

The historic Tokeland Hotel and Restaurant (circa 1894), off Kindred Avenue, provides local accommodations and dining (open 7:30 a.m. to 8:00 p.m. daily). Be sure to call ahead for hotel or dining reservations (360-267-7006).

Return to SR 105 and go right toward Raymond. Continue along the north shore of Willapa Bay with its mudflats, salt marshes, and adjoining coniferous and broadleaf forests. Check the **Cedar and North Rivers** and the bay for migrating Greater White-fronted and Snow Geese in fall and grebes and waterfowl in winter. The mouth of the North River can be a good spot for migrating shorebirds on a rising and falling tide.

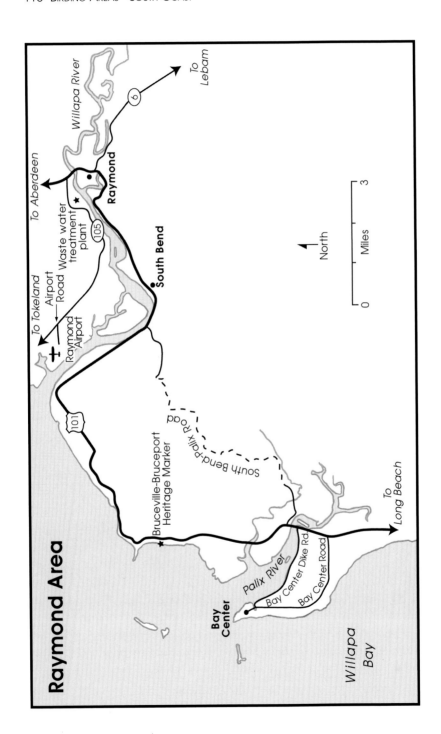

Raymond Area

Raymond Area

At MP 4.5, turn south on Airport Road to the Willapa Harbor Airport, a.k.a. **Raymond Airport**. In the past, White-tailed Kites had been seen on the top of the evergreen trees surrounding the airport runway. More recent sightings of White-tailed Kites have occurred east of Lebam, the Julia Butler Hansen Refuge, the Chinook Valley Road, and Puget Island. Occasionally, large elk herds are visible near the runway.

Raymond Airport   Bob Morse

Watch for roosting shorebirds at the airport during high tide and nearby Palm Warbler (rare, fall and winter). In winter, check the small freshwater ponds and sloughs along Highway 105 near the airport for Pied-billed Grebe, Eurasian and American Wigeons, Green-winged Teal, Ring-necked Duck, Lesser Scaup, and Bufflehead. Also in winter, watch for falcons, Northern Rough-legged Hawk, and Northern Shrike.

Continue east on SR 105 toward Raymond. Just past MP 1, the **City of Raymond Waste Water Treatment Plant** on the right, is a good place in winter to check for scaup, Ruddy Duck, and Mew Gull. The treatment plant is closed to the public so view the birds from outside the fence.

In Raymond, take US 101 south toward South Bend. Stop in **Raymond** if a rest stop or espresso is needed. Restrooms are available at a city park along the river (closed in winter) by going left (east) on Franklin Street or at the Visitor Center by going right (west) on Commercial Street. For a cup of coffee, try the Espresso Drive-Through, just east of US 101 at Commercial Street. Take a few moments to enjoy the roadside iron sculptures erected along US 101 in Raymond. There are places to grab a bite to eat at the south end of Raymond along US 101. Watch for Western Scrub-Jay in the residential parts of town.

To look for White-tailed Kite in **Lebam**, turn left on SR 6 in Raymond and travel about 14 miles to Lebam. At MP 16.2, east of Lebam, the Elk Prairie Road has been productive for kites in the past.

Seven miles west of Lebam, a surprisingly White Ibis spent part of January 2001 at the Crawford Diary foraging in the cow pastures for worms and grubs.

Continue south on US 101 along the picturesque Willapa (pronounced "Will' apa") River (picnic tables) through **South Bend**, the "Oyster Capitol of the World." Watch for Purple Martin in season along the Willapa River. If you missed the Raymond Espresso stand, try Gardiner's on the left in South Bend.

In South Bend, there are two routes south. The main route is US 101. The alternate route is a 9 mile road (6 miles on dirt) through higher elevations and old clear cuts. To take the alternate route, turn left on Willapa Avenue in South Bend which soon becomes the **South Bend-Palix Road**. Follow the road into the higher hills with logging roads leading into managed coniferous forests of varying ages. Most of the logging roads are gated but foot travel will gain access to places where Common Nighthawk and Gray Jay have been seen (uncommon in Pacific County). Northern Saw-whet Owl may be heard in evening at the edge of clear cuts along this road. The moist creek bottoms have moss draped stands of red alder with a thick fern understory. The alternate route joins US 101 north of the Palix River.

To take the US 101 route, continue through South Bend. South of town, check the open farmlands for flocks of wintering Canada Geese (including different subspecies), Eurasian and American Wigeons, and gulls, especially Mew and Ring-billed. Cattle Egret and Tropical Kingbird have on rare occasion been seen in this area from late fall to early winter.

Continue south along US 101. The pullout at the **Bruceville-Bruceport Heritage Marker** at MP 46.2 offers an outlook over Willapa Bay. Check for migrating waterfowl, especially American Wigeon, which can be abundant in fall and winter, and the occasional Eurasian Wigeon. This spot can be good for migrating shorebirds on rising and falling tides.

Just south of the **Palix River**, turn west onto **Bay Center-Dike Road**. When the fields to the south of the road are flooded in the winter, search for Eurasian Wigeon among the large flocks of American Wigeon. Wintering Canada Geese (check for different subspecies), Dunlin, and Mew Gull often frequent these open fields. The sloughs and shallow ponds in the fields may hold Green-winged Teal, Lesser Scaup, Bufflehead, or even a Great Egret (uncommon, fall and winter) or Snowy Egret (rare, spring) or White Ibis (same bird seen near Lebam in January 2001). Large flocks of shorebirds, especially Black-bellied Plover and Dunlin, may be here during spring migration (late April). Scan the Palix River from the bridge to the river mouth for Red-throated and Common Loons, Pied-billed, Horned, Western, and Clark's (very rare) Grebes, Greater Scaup, Bufflehead, and Red-breasted Merganser. The best time to bird the river is usually an hour or so before or after high tide. When in Bay Center, take Bay Center Road south back to US 101.

Continue south on US 101 as it winds through the managed forests of Douglas fir and western hemlock separated by occasional clear cuts and freshwater creeks as they enter the salt water marshes of Willapa Bay.

At the junction of US 101 and SR 4 (MP 28.9), turn right towards Long Beach Peninsula. Here the road follows the Naselle River with its open, expansive marshes.

Willapa National Wildlife Refuge

The Refuge Headquarters for the 13,900 acre Willapa National Wildlife Refuge is located past MP 25 on the left. Near the refuge headquarters, at dawn, from mid April to mid September, Marbled Murrelet may be heard passing overhead to and from their nesting sites in the old growth forests of the Willapa Hills. A boat launch across the road from the refuge headquarters allows those with a boat to gain easy access to

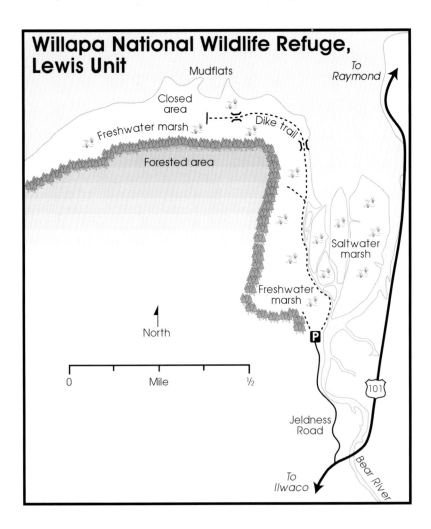

nearby Long Island and other parts of **Willapa Bay**. Willapa Bay is a popular spot for kayaking along the South Coast.

Long Island, the largest estuarine island along the Pacific Coast, has 5,460 acres of saltgrass tidal marsh, intertidal mudflats, and a native forest of western red cedar, western hemlock, and Sitka spruce. A 274 acre Cedar Grove is one of the last remnants of the old growth coastal forest that was once prevalent along the coast. These woods host Bald Eagle, Ruffed and Blue Grouse, Marbled Murrelet (common nester), Red-breasted Sapsucker, Pileated Woodpecker, as well as Roosevelt elk, black-tailed deer, beaver, river otter, and the most concentrated population of black bear in North America. Nesting Band-tailed Pigeon can usually be seen from May through September. The west side of Long Island, with its large area of eelgrass habitat, provides an important food source for large flocks of wintering and migrating Brant.

After crossing Greenhead Slough, check the open water of the salt marsh on the right for Red-throated Loon, Western Grebe, Double-crested Cormorant, Great Blue Heron, assorted subspecies of Canada Goose, Canvasback, Greater Scaup, Bufflehead, and Common Merganser. Watch for perched or soaring Bald Eagle, Northern Harrier, and Red-tailed Hawk.

Beyond MP 19, check for Roosevelt Elk in the open meadows on the left, particularly at dawn or dusk.

The entrance to the **Lewis Unit of the Willapa National Wildlife Refuge** is on the right, just past Bear River on Jeldness Road. Park in the small parking lot at the end of the road. There are two trails from here that can be used to explore the refuge. The path on the left (stay right at the fork after the gate) in a few hundred yards reaches an expansive freshwater marsh with good numbers of wintering waterfowl.

The other trail leads to the right from the parking lot along a long dike to the south end of Willapa Bay. West of the dike is a freshwater marsh while the east-side of the dike has a salt water marsh. The dike trail extends about 1½ miles before the closed section of the Lewis Unit is reached. Along

Salt water marsh at Lewis Unit, Willapa NWR

Bob Morse

the way, there are two bridges over sloughs to allow access to the mudflats of Willapa Bay.

The marshes here and the adjoining mudflats provide excellent wintering habitat for Canada Goose, Brant, American Wigeon, Northern Pintail, Green-winged Teal, Canvasback, Greater and Lesser Scaups, Bufflehead, and Red-breasted and Common Mergansers. American Bittern and Virginia Rails nest here. Large numbers of migrating shorebirds can be seen from the dike in spring and fall. White-fronted and Snow Geese pass through in April during spring migration. Trumpeter Swans regularly winter in the Lewis Unit. Look for Western Kingbird (rare), Yellow-headed Blackbird (rare in Pacific County), and a variety of wintering sparrows including a few records for Swamp Sparrow. This has been one of the more consistent locations for wintering Swamp Sparrow in Washington.

Parts of the Lewis and Riekkola Units of the refuge may have active waterfowl hunting between early-October and late-January.

Riekkola Unit, Willapa NWR   Bob Morse

Continue southwest on US 101 toward the Long Beach Peninsula. Continue straight (do not use Alternate US 101 at MP 15.8). To reach the **Riekkola Unit of the Willapa National Wildlife Refuge**, turn right at the first blinking light onto Sandridge Road. Turn right onto 67th Place and follow this road 2.4 miles past the cranberry bogs and mixed conifer and broadleaf forest of the Long Beach watershed to a parking area and gated entrance to the refuge. Check the large flocks of Canada Geese for different subspecies including Western, Cackling, Vancouver/Dusky, Taverner's, or the rarer Aleutian subspecies. A rare Emperor or Snow Goose may winter in the farmlands here.

Return to and continue north along Sandridge Road. Take a right onto **85th Street** to check the newly developed refuge wetlands on the left. These shallow ponds and surrounding fields may have Canada Geese, American Wigeon, Green-winged Teal, as well as Killdeer. In winter, check for Golden-crowned Sparrow in the bushes at the intersection of 85th Street and Sandridge Road.

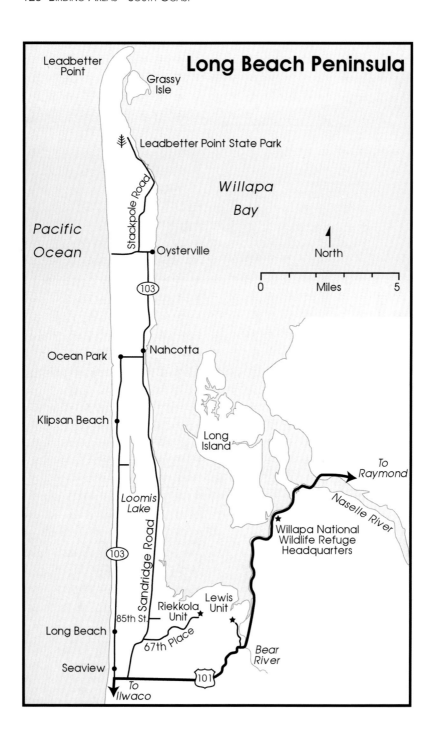

Long Beach Peninsula

Leadbetter Point

Grassy Isle

Leadbetter Point State Park

Willapa Bay

Pacific Ocean

Stackpole Road

Oysterville

North

103

0   Miles   5

Nahcotta

Ocean Park

Klipsan Beach

Long Island

To Raymond

Naselle River

Loomis Lake

Willapa National Wildlife Refuge Headquarters

Sandridge Road

103

Lewis Unit

Riekkola Unit

85th St.

Long Beach

67th Place

Bear River

Seaview

101

To Ilwaco

Long Beach Peninsula

Continue north on Sandridge Road. In the town of **Nahcotta**, the Washington Department of Fish & Wildlife's Nahcotta Tidelands Interpretive Site is on the right. Check the nearby blackberries for wintering White-crowned and Golden-crowned Sparrows. Turn right at 273rd Street in Nahcotta. One of every six oysters eaten in the U.S. comes from Willapa Bay. Nahcotta is famous for its Willapa Bay oysters and the Willapa Bay Interpretive Center here describes the history of the local 150 year old oyster industry. Check the marina, oyster and seafood plants, rock jetty, and nearby waters for Common Loon, Red-necked and Western Grebes, Brown Pelican (summer and fall), Great Blue Heron, Ruddy and Black Turnstones, Surfbird, Herring Gull (winter), and Glaucous Gull (rare in winter). The Ark Restaurant and Bakery has excellent cuisine. Some rock shorebirds and gulls may be searching through the mounds of oyster shells near the restaurant. Also check the waters around the boat basin at the end of 275th Street.

Farther north along Sandridge Road, bear right at Territory Road to visit the National Historical District of Oysterville and see many of the original houses built in the 1860's and 1870's. Turn left onto the Oysterville Road which goes west across the peninsula. Just past the Oysterville store, turn left into the **Oysterville Cemetery** which can be productive for passerines, especially during migration. Continue west on Oysterville Road and turn north (right) onto Stackpole Road to get to Leadbetter Point.

Leadbetter Point

Leadbetter State Park, a day-use natural area, is located three miles north of Oysterville along Stackpole Road. The Willapa National Wildlife Refuge manages the land at the tip of the Long Beach Peninsula, including **Leadbetter Point**. This is a land of shifting sand dunes, expansive sandy beaches, small shrubs, saltwater marshes, and Sitka spruce

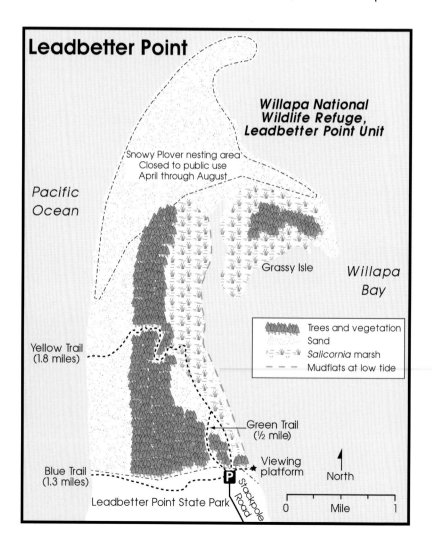

Leadbetter Point

Willapa National Wildlife Refuge, Leadbetter Point Unit

Snowy Plover nesting area
Closed to public use
April through August

Pacific Ocean

Grassy Isle

Willapa Bay

Trees and vegetation
Sand
Salicornia marsh
Mudflats at low tide

Yellow Trail
(1.8 miles)

Green Trail
(½ mile)

Blue Trail
(1.3 miles)

Viewing platform

North

Leadbetter Point State Park

Stackpole Road

0   Mile   1

forests. There are trails from the parking area to the sandy beach to the west, to a viewing platform to the east, as well as an interpretive loop trail. **Note**: the trails may be flooded through the rainy season (October through April).

In the open areas north of the parking lot, search the tops of conifers in fall and winter for White-tailed Kite. On the east-side, a salt marsh of Pickleweed (*Salicornia*) and Arrowgrass (*Triglochin*) floods and drains twice daily with the change of tides. These rich salt marshes are an important feeding and nesting habitat for Brant, especially during April and May when thousands stop here on their northward migration.

Almost all of the shorebirds regularly found along the Washington coast can be seen at Leadbetter Point in the salt marshes or tidal flats. Sandpipers such as Black-bellied and Semipalmated Plovers, Greater Yellowlegs, Ruddy Turnstone, Sanderling, Western and Least Sandpipers, Dunlin, and Short-billed Dowitcher are common in spring and fall. Spring migration brings large numbers of Western Sandpiper, Dunlin, and Short-billed Dowitcher. Check for American and Pacific Golden-Plovers in fall (both uncommon). A Curlew Sandpiper spent four days on the west side of Leadbetter Point in early August 2000 and a Little Curlew was reported in May 2001. Best shorebird viewing is on an incoming tide.

Snowy Plover nest at the tip of Leadbetter Point in a clearly-marked, restricted area. Do not enter this area. It may be possible to see Snowy Plover along the west side of the point south of the restricted area.

In the *Salicornia* marsh, Pectoral Sandpiper are evident in fall and Sharp-tailed Sandpiper are occasionally found with them just west of Grassy Isle from late September to late October.

Grassy Isle is a stand of willows, alders, and shrubs near the tip of Leadbetter Point. There is no trail to Grassy Isle. From the parking lot, take the path east to the observation platform, follow along the shore to the north tip of the point, and then on to Grassy Isle. It is a long, arduous trek and taking shortcuts may mean having to backtrack to cross the sloughs. This area is prone to flooding especially from October to April and rubber boots are recommended. Hip boots may be required depending on the amount of recent rains.

East side of Leadbetter Point with   Bob Morse
Grassy Isle in right background

In the spring and especially fall (during the second and third week of September) Grassy Isle can host unusual migrating passerines (Magnolia Warbler, September 1974). Leadbetter Point also has its share of rarities – Gray-tailed Tattler, Bristle-thighed Curlew (May 1982), Hudsonian and Bar-tailed Godwits.

In invasion years, check for Snowy Owl at the tip of Leadbetter Point. In winter, watch for Merlin, Peregrine Falcon, Gyrfalcon, and Snow Bunting along stretches of the upper beach.

Relatively under-birded, Leadbetter Point is an area of great potential. One is never sure what may turn up and the possibilities make for exciting birding.

After birding Leadbetter Point, return to Sandridge Road. Continue south on Sandridge Road and, at Bay Avenue, follow SR103 west and then south through the towns of Ocean Park, Klipsan Beach, Long Beach, and Seaview with their variety of motels, restaurants, galleries, gift shops, antique stores, and amusement centers. Along the way, take a left onto 188th Place to access **Loomis Lake** which may have good numbers of wintering grebes and waterfowl*. At Long Beach, a right at the traffic light will allow access to the "World's Longest Beach". The Shelburne Inn in Seaview offers fine accommodations and marvelous food.

* A Washington Department of Fish and Wildlife Access Stewardship Decal is needed to park here. Information about obtaining a decal is provided in the More Coastal Information Appendix.

Long Beach Peninsula
kite flying

beachdog.com

The Long Beach Peninsula Visitor Information Center is located at the junction of US 101 and SR 103 in Seaview. At this intersection, continue south on US 101 towards Ilwaco. At 1 1/4 miles on the left, freshwater **Black Lake** usually has Pied-billed Grebe, Canada Goose, increasing numbers of wintering Trumpeter Swan, Mallard, American Coot, bathing gulls, and a covered picnic area.

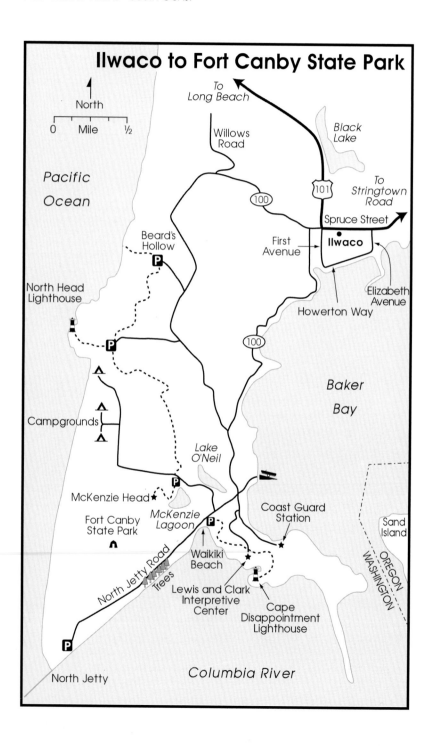

Ilwaco to Fort Canby State Park

Ilwaco

At the southern end of the Long Beach Peninsula sits the town of **Ilwaco**, home to charter, sports, and commercial fishing. At Spruce Street in Ilwaco (the only traffic light), turn right on SR Loop 100. Follow the signs toward the Fort Canby State Park and the North Head Lighthouse.

In a little less than a mile, **Willows Road**, on the right, offers good birding in mixed broadleaf and coniferous woods, especially during migration. Pull well off to the right or go a little way downhill to park. Return to SR Loop 100 and turn right.

One-half mile further, a pullout on the right provides a commanding view of **Beard's Hollow** with its network of ponds and marshes. At the bottom of the hill, there is a parking lot for Beard's Hollow. The woods on the south side of the parking area can be productive for coniferous forest birds while the open spruce and broadleaf woods and wetlands to the north and west can have woodpeckers, Red-breasted Sapsucker, flycatchers, and warblers in season. There are trails here to the North Head Lighthouse and the ocean beach.

Continue along SR Loop 100. At 0.6 miles further, turn right to the **North Head Lighthouse**. Park in the parking lot and walk 0.2 miles to the lighthouse. Migrant passerines are common, during spring and fall, on the south-west facing slope of shrubby thickets and mixed coniferous and broadleaf woods.

Besides great views, search for migrating Gray Whale (spring), Brown Pelican (spring through fall), and passing Sooty Shearwater (summer and fall). Scoters and other diving ducks and Pigeon Guillemot are usually in the offshore waters. Black Oystercatcher and Surfbird may be on the rocks below the lighthouse.

A 1.6 mile trail leads through mixed broadleaf woods from the lighthouse parking lot to Fort Canby State Park.

Return to SR Loop 100 and turn right to Fort Canby State Park.

Fort Canby State Park

The 1,700 acre Fort Canby State Park, located at the mouth of the Columbia River, offers 250 campsites with 89 RV hookups. It has a wide variety of habitats including open salt water, rock jetty, rocky cliffs, sandy ocean beach, freshwater lakes and marshes, salt water marsh, coniferous and broadleaf forests, shrubby thickets, and park-like settings. Several trails of varying lengths offer many opportunities to bird the woods of the park.

Fort Canby campground   Bob Morse

After passing the entrance booth, go right into the campground. Freshwater **Lake O'Neil** and McKenzie Lagoon, in the center of the park, usually have Pied-billed Grebe, occasional wintering swans, and ducks. A ¹/₂ mile trail leaves from the **McKenzie Head** parking lot to a high spot overlooking **McKenzie Lagoon**, the ocean, and state park.

The 1.6 mile trail to the North Head Lighthouse is on the right past the McKenzie Head parking lot. The trail winds past freshwater marshes and bluffs before climbing the 200 foot high bluff to the lighthouse parking lot. In the first one-half mile section, before it climbs up hill, a pair of courting Northern Pygmy-Owls was seen in October 1993. Hutton's Vireo can be seen. Winter Wren and Golden-crowned Kinglet are common here.

Check the broadleaf trees surrounding the **campgrounds** and nearby thickets in the park for Bewick's Wren, warblers (in season), and Spotted Towhee. Camping sites 1-180, among the 30 foot tall conifers, offer Chestnut-backed Chickadee, Red-breasted Nuthatch, Bewick's Wren, Golden-crowned and Ruby-crowned Kinglets (latter, winter), and Townsend's Warbler (uncommon, winter).

North Jetty   Keith Brady

Take the North Jetty Road to the rock jetty and check the isolated conifers along the south side of the road for passerines during migration. Watch for raptors. The **North Jetty** of the Columbia River is subject to constant winter storms that change access to the jetty, cut away beach front, and deposit logs along access roads and parking lots. Drive to the end of the jetty road, then walk out along the rock jetty to view long strings of passing Pacific and Common Loons, Sooty Shearwater (summer and fall), Surf and White-winged Scoters, and Black-legged Kittiwake (uncommon). Search for Common and Arctic Terns (rare) during migration. Watch for jaegers, with Parasitic being the most likely, in fall and spring migration. Northern Fulmar and Short-tailed Shearwater have been seen from the end of the jetty from November through January. Look for Wandering Tattler (spring and fall), Black Turnstone, and Surfbird among the jetty rocks. The jetty is recommended at low or receding tides because of the extreme spray, tidal wash, and treacherous walking during higher tides. Watch out for sneaker waves , which can wash the unwary off the jetty.

A Mountain Plover spent part of the winter 2000-2001 at the edge of the dune grasses just north of the jetty.

Marbled Murrelet have nested in the mature moss draped conifers in the state park and in similar habitats on the peninsula from Fort Canby State Park to the North Head Lighthouse back to Ilwaco.

Across from the entrance to the Fort Canby State Park, an access road leads to a **boat launch** into Baker Bay. In this area, a pair of Yellow-billed Loons spent part of the winter of 1993-1994. Common Loon, Red-necked and Western Grebe, Greater Scaup and Bufflehead often inhabit these waters while Double-crested and Pelagic Cormorants perch on nearby pilings.

The **Cape Disappointment Lighthouse** (the oldest lighthouse still in use on the West Coast) and the **Lewis and Clark Interpretive Center** offer great views of the Columbia River as it meets the Pacific Ocean. Take a few moments to experience the adventure of the Lewis and Clark Expedition as illustrated in the interpretive center exhibits (open 10:00 a.m. to 5:00 p.m. daily except in winter when it closes at 4:00 p.m.). Brandt's and Pelagic Cormorants, Glaucous-winged Gull, and Pigeon Guillemot nest on the cliffs below the interpretive center. Use caution and stay behind the fence. Some of the better views of the cliffs are from Waikiki Beach or from the North Jetty Road parking lot.

Cape Disappointment   Wayne O'Neil

Ilwaco to Naselle

Return to **Ilwaco** and turn right at the traffic light onto First Avenue. After the road turns left and becomes Howerton Avenue, check the roof and the grounds around Jessie's Ilwaco Fish Company for wintering gulls. Continue down the road and go right at the stop sign (the docks will then be on the right). Search the grassy area on the left for shorebirds at high tide in fall and winter. Black Turnstone are sometimes on the docks. Scan the waters off the **marina** for loons and grebes, especially Eared Grebe in winter and the pilings for eagles and gulls. Purple Martin nest in the pilings near the marina. Return to US 101 by going north 2 blocks on Elizabeth Avenue (do not take Howerton Avenue). Turn right at Spruce Street (US 101).

Ilwaco marina   Bob Morse

Continue on US 101 1.7 miles, and turn right on the **Stringtown Road** (it's easy to miss the sign). The small airport on the left has Bald Eagle, Horned Lark (winter), Lapland Longspur (fall and winter), and Western Meadowlark. Merlin hunt along the road. Baker Bay, on the right, can have seasonally good numbers of shorebirds on an incoming tide.

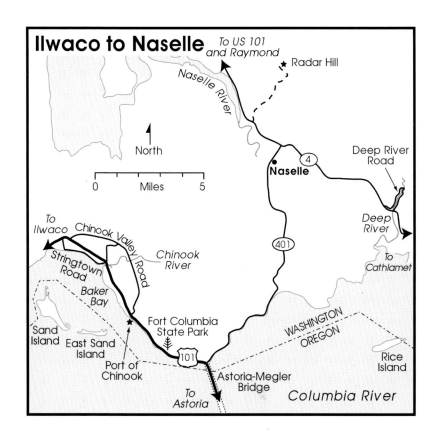

Ilwaco to Naselle

To US 101 and Raymond

Naselle River

Radar Hill

North

0   Miles   5

Naselle

4

Deep River Road

Deep River

To Ilwaco

Chinook Valley Road

Stringtown Road

Chinook River

401

To Cathlamet

Baker Bay

Fort Columbia State Park

WASHINGTON
OREGON

Sand Island

East Sand Island

Port of Chinook

101

Rice Island

Astoria-Megler Bridge

To Astoria

Columbia River

Check the hummingbird feeders at the last house on the road (No. 74) for Rufous Hummingbird in spring and summer and Anna's Hummingbird in winter.

The **Chinook River** (where the Stringtown Road re-meets Highway 101) has shorebirds in fall and hundreds of ducks (most abundant are Mallard, Northern Pintail, and American Wigeon) in fall and winter on an incoming tide although they may be scarce during the hunting season. Good viewpoints are across from the Elkhorn Truss plant and on the right as the Springtown Road meets US 101 at the bridge. Search for egrets (rare) and herons in the marsh along the river.

Cross US 101 and proceed straight onto Chinook Dike Road. Continue by open fields lined with shrubby thickets which hold sparrows in winter. At the "T" intersection, turn right onto **Chinook Valley Road** and at the next "T" intersection (2.8 miles further), go left continuing on Chinook Valley Road. A Fork-tailed Flycatcher was seen at this intersection in September, 1995. This area is good for geese, ducks, Black-bellied Plover, yellowlegs, and sometimes phalarope, especially at high tide or during and after rainstorms. In winter, check shrubby thickets for "Sooty" Fox, Song, Golden-crowned and White-crowned Sparrow. The Chinook Valley Road is an important area for wintering raptors. Look for White-tailed Kite (possible nester), Bald Eagle, Northern Harrier, Sharp-shinned, Cooper's, Red-tailed and Rough-legged (winter) Hawks, and Northern Shrike. Continue less than a mile to the intersection with US 101.

At US 101, turn left (east). Turn right at the **Port of Chinook** sign and check the harbor, jetty, and waters off the marina for loons and grebes. The Caspian Tern colony on East Sand Island can be seen to the west.

East Sand Island has been a subject of recent controversy regarding its use by Caspian Terns. Historically, Caspian Terns have nested in Willapa Bay and Grays Harbor. But, as the terns gradually lost habitat due to dredging, vegetation growth, and predatory birds, they arrived at Rice Island, 20 miles up the Columbia River where the Army Corps of Engineers had been placing their dredge spoils. Near Rice Island, the Caspian Terns found millions of migrating juvenile salmon an easy food source, devouring an estimated 11 million salmon smolts in 1998. In 1999 and 2000, workers cleared the vegetation from East Sand Island in an attempt to relocate the nesting Caspian Terns away from the Rice Island migrating smolts. A lawsuit by National Audubon Society, Seattle Audubon Society, among others called for the Corps of Engineers to stop destroying tern breeding habitat and tern eggs at Rice Island until the agency conducted an Environmental Impact Statement. Meanwhile, the Caspian Terns found the dredge spoils of East Sand Island to their liking and have abandoned Rice Island.

At **Fort Columbia State Park**, pull off the road to look over

Baker Bay and check the sandbars for shorebirds and the pilings for Bald Eagle. Pileated Woodpecker may be found near the parking lot and buildings at Fort Columbia State Park and breeding Hammond's Flycatcher and Varied Thrush have been noted along the trail above the youth hostel. Marbled Murrelet have nested in the moss draped mature conifers in the park.

Proceed east on Highway 101 toward the Astoria-Megler Bridge. Take a moment to visit the Lewis and Clark Heritage Markers along the highway.

At the Astoria-Megler Bridge, stay on the Washington side of the river and proceed north on Highway 401, passing the Megler Visitor Area with its picnic tables and restrooms.

At Naselle, to get into the higher elevations of the Willapa Hills, turn left onto SR 4 (west). In about 1.7 miles, turn right at the sign towards the Naselle Youth Camp but take the left branch that heads to the West Lakes Recreation Area and **Radar Hill**. Follow the main road, passing by turnoffs to the Lakes, about 4 miles (with some rough stretches of road) to reach the top of Radar Hill, at 1,995 foot elevation. On a clear day, expect to see the tops of Mt. Rainier, Mt. St. Helens, Mt. Adams, the Columbia River and the Long Beach Peninsula. Birds of the area include Common Nighthawk, Gray Jay, and Varied Thrush.

Return to SR 4, turn left, and continue east toward the town of **Cathlamet**. After crossing the Deep River, turn left (north) at MP 11.0 on **East Deep River Road** for a 3-mile loop through broadleaf and occasional coniferous woods and shrubby thickets adjoining the Deep River with neighboring freshwater marshes. Check for ducks, raptors, woodpeckers, wrens, other passerines, and wintering sparrows. Bear left, cross Deep River, and return to SR 4 along the west side of Deep River.

Julia Butler Hansen Refuge for Columbian White-tailed Deer

SR 4 continues east through hills of managed Douglas fir and western hemlock forests of varying ages. On SR 4, east of

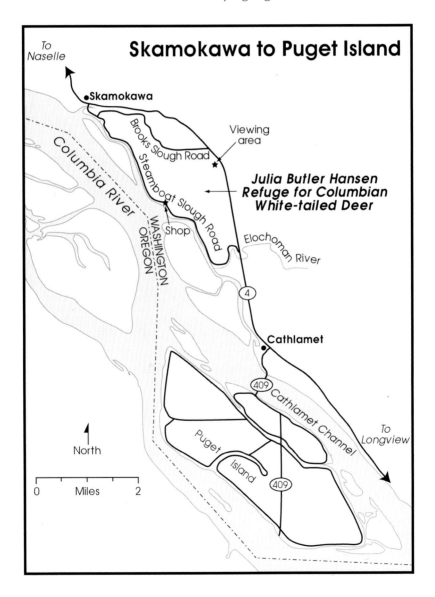

Skamokawa to Puget Island

Skamokawa, stop at the Viewing Area at the **Julia Butler Hansen Refuge for the Columbian White-tailed Deer** to look for endangered Columbian White-tailed Deer (best viewed between September and May).

Julia Butler Hansen NWR   Bob Morse

Further along SR 4, take **Steamboat Slough Road**, a 7 mile loop road, for other views of the refuge and its pasturelands intermixed with sloughs, rivers, and broadleaf woods. The Elochoman River, on the left, often has numbers of waterfowl, including Tundra Swan, Wood Duck, Redhead, and a few records of Tufted Duck in winter. With proper tides, the cove in front of a shop/warehouse (on the right) can provide good views of Tundra Swan, ducks, and shorebirds in winter. Proceeding past the shop, check the Columbia River (on the left) for Pied-billed, Red-necked, Eared (winter), and Western Grebes, Hooded, Red-breasted, and Common Mergansers, and other waterfowl.

On the right, the open fields may have Greater White-fronted, Snow, and Canada Geese (including the Dusky subspecies), Tundra Swan, White-tailed Kite, Red-tailed Hawk, Greater and Lesser Yellowlegs, several species of peep, dowitchers, and occasional Short-eared Owl. From fall through spring, Sharp-shinned, Cooper's, and Rough-legged Hawks, Merlin, and Peregrine Falcon may be hunting these fields. American Bittern, Bald Eagle, Northern Harrier, and American Kestrel may be seen. Continuing along Steamboat Slough Road expect to see Great Blue Heron, Red-winged and Brewer's Blackbirds as well as Northern Shrike in season and good numbers of wintering sparrows including Golden-crowned. Watch for Columbian White-tailed Deer in the open fields and near edges of the woods. Pause at the intersection with the first paved road to the right and check the Purple Martin boxes on the pilings around the dock of the house on the slough. Take the paved road here to the right (Brooks Slough Road) to return to SR 4.

Puget Island

At Cathlamet, turn right onto SR 409, pass through the small town of **Cathlamet**, and proceed over the bridge to **Puget Island**. Puget Island, in the middle of the Columbia River, consists mostly of open pastureland with sloughs bordered by stands of alder and shrubby thickets. Drive the roads along the perimeter of the island (less traffic) for good views of the river and dairy farms. The rivers and sloughs have American Wigeon (watch for Eurasian), Gadwall, Mallard, and both scaups. The wet fields and edges have Great Blue Heron, Killdeer, Common Snipe, and the drier fields host wintering Canada Goose (check for different subspecies). The tall trees overlooking the fields, sloughs, and the river may have White-tailed Kite, Bald Eagle, Red-tailed and Rough-legged (winter) Hawks. Search for chickadees, wrens, Spotted Towhee, and sparrows in the thickets. Western Scrub-Jay are common here.

Return to SR 4 and go east towards Kelso and Longview. The road passes by impressive basalt cliffs, parallels the Columbia River, and travels through thick stands of Douglas fir, western red cedar, and red alder with a lush understory of ferns and salal. Cliff Swallow nest on the basalt cliffs on either side of the County Line Park.

REFERENCES

Buckley, C. 1991. *Welcome to Washington*. REMIS, Bellevue, Washington..

Debenedictis, P. A. 1995. Red Crossbills, One Through Eight. *Birding* 28:494-501.

Groth, J. 1996. *Crossbills Audiovisual Guide*, American Museum of Natural History at: http://research.amnh.org/ornithology/crossbills/.

Komer, P. D. 1998. *The Pacific Northwest Coast*. Duke University Press, Durham and London.

May, A. & E. 2000. *Northwest Coast*. Longstreet Press, Marietta, Georgia.

McNulty, T. 1996. *Olympic National Park*, A Natural History. Houghton Mifflin, New York.

Mlodinow, S. 1993. Finding the Pacific Golden-Plover in North America. *Birding* 25: 322 – 329.

Mlodinow, S. G. and M. O'Brien. 1996. *America's 100 Most Wanted Birds*. Falcon Press, Helena, Montana.

Mlodinow, S. 1997. The Long-billed Murrelet. *Birding* 29: 461 – 475.

Morse, R. W. 1994. *A Birder's Guide to Ocean Shores, Washington*. R. W. Morse Company, Olympia, Washington. (out of print)

Paulson, D. R. 1993. *Shorebirds of the Pacific Northwest.* University of Washington Press, Seattle, Washington, 406 p.

Sibley, D. 2000. *National Audubon Society, The Sibley Guide to Birds.* A.A. Knopf, New York.

Spring, I. And Manning, H. 1998. *100 Hikes in Washington's South Cascades and Olympics.* The Mountaineers, Seattle, Washington.

Wahl, T. R. and Paulson, D. R. 1991. *A Guide to Bird Finding in Washington.* Print Shop, Lynden, Washington.

Zimmer, K. J. 1985. *The Western Bird Watcher.* Prentice-Hall, Englewood Cliffs, New Jersey.

Zink, R.M. and Kessen, A.E. 1999. Species Limits in the Fox Sparrow. *Birding* 31: 508-517.

APPENDICES

CHECKLIST OF COASTAL BIRDS

CHECKLIST OF COASTAL WASHINGTON BIRDS

Date _____ Time _____

Locality _____

Observers _____

Weather _____ No. Species _____

This checklist covers the birds of coastal Washington from the
Strait of Juan de Fuca to the Columbia River, up to 30 miles inland.

Seasons		
	Spring	March, April, May
	Summer	June, July
	Fall	August, September, October, November
	Winter	December, January, February

Frequency		
	C - Common	likely to be found on 75% to 100% of trips to suitable habitat
	U - Uncommon	likely to be found on 25% to 75% of trips to suitable habitat
	R - Rare	likely to be found on less than 25% of trips to suitable habitat
	X - Accidental	fewer than 15 records
	I - Irregular	occurs on irregular basis in suitable habitat
	L - Local	occurs locally
	P - Pelagic	pelagic species (rarely seen from shore)

Species recorded less than five times are shown in the back of the checklist. Solid lines separate orders, dotted lines separate families.

Species	Season S S F W
Red-throated Loon	C U C C
Pacific Loon	C U C C
Common Loon	C U C C
Yellow-billed Loon	X X X R
Pied-billed Grebe	C C C C
Horned Grebe	C R C C
Red-necked Grebe	C R C C
Eared Grebe	R - R R
Western Grebe	C R C C
Clark's Grebe	X - X X
Black-footed Albatross(P)	C C C U
Laysan Albatross(P)	R X R U
Northern Fulmar(P)	C U C C
Mottled Petrel(P)	X - X X
Murphy's Petrel(P)	X - X -
Pink-footed Shearwater(P)	C C C X
Flesh-footed Shearwater(P)	U U U -
Buller's Shearwater(P)	- R C -
Sooty Shearwater	C C C R
Short-tailed Shearwater(P)	U - U U
Manx Shearwater (P)	X X X -
Fork-tailed Storm-Petrel(P)	C C C R
Leach's Storm-Petrel(P)	U U X -
Brown Pelican	R C C X

Species	Season S S F W
Double-crested Cormorant	C C C C
Brandt's Cormorant	C C C U
Pelagic Cormorant	C C C C
American Bittern	U U U R
Great Blue Heron	C C C C
Great Egret	X X U U
Snowy Egret	X X X -
Cattle Egret(I)	- - R R
Green Heron	U U U R
Black-crowned Night-Heron	- - R R
Turkey Vulture	C C C R
Gr. White-fronted Goose	U X U U
Emperor Goose	X - X X
Snow Goose	R - R R
Canada Goose	C C C C
Brant	C R U U
Trumpeter Swan	C X C C
Tundra Swan	U - U U
Wood Duck	U U U R
Gadwall	C C C C
Eurasian Wigeon	U - U U
American Wigeon	C R C C
Mallard	C C C C
Blue-winged Teal	U C C R
Cinnamon Teal	U U U X

Species	Season S S F W
Northern Shoveler	C C C U
Northern Pintail	C R C C
Green-winged Teal	C R C C
Canvasback	U X U U
Redhead	R X R R
Ring-necked Duck	C R C C
Tufted Duck	X - X X
Greater Scaup	C R C C
Lesser Scaup	C R C C
Harlequin Duck(L)	C C C C
Surf Scoter	C U C C
White-winged Scoter	C U C C
Black Scoter(L)	C R C C
Long-tailed Duck(L)	U X U U
Bufflehead	C R C C
Common Goldeneye	C - C C
Barrow's Goldeneye	U - U U
Hooded Merganser	C U C C
Red-breasted Merganser	C R C C
Common Merganser	C C C C
Ruddy Duck	C R C C
Osprey	C C C X
White-tailed Kite(L)	U U U U
Bald Eagle	C C C C
Northern Harrier(shinned)	C U C C
Sharp-shinned Hawk	U R U U
Cooper's Hawk	U R U U
Northern Goshawk	R R R R
Red-tailed Hawk	C C C C
Rough-legged Hawk	U - U U
Golden Eagle(L)	R R R R
American Kestrel	U U U U
Merlin	U R U U
Peregrine Falcon	U U U U
Gyrfalcon	X - R R
Ring-necked Pheasant	C C C C
Ruffed Grouse	U U U U
Blue Grouse	U U U U
Wild Turkey (L, Introduced)	R R R R
Mountain Quail(L)	R R R R
Virginia Rail	C C C U
Sora	U U U X
American Coot	C U C C
Sandhill Crane	R - R X
Black-bellied Plover	C U C C
Pacific Golden-Plover	R R U X
American Golden-Plover	X R U -
Snowy Plover(L)	U U U R
Semipalmated Plover	C C C U

Species	Season S S F W
Killdeer	C C C C
Black Oystercatcher(L)	U U U U
Black-necked Stilt	X - X -
American Avocet	X - X X
Greater Yellowlegs	C U C U
Lesser Yellowlegs	R R U X
Solitary Sandpiper	X X X -
Willet(L)	U R U U
Wandering Tattler	C U C X
Spotted Sandpiper	U U U R
Whimbrel	C C C R
Bristle-thighed Curlew	X - - -
Long-billed Curlew	R R U U
Hudsonian Godwit	X - X -
Bar-tailed Godwit(L)	X X R -
Marbled Godwit	U R U U
Ruddy Turnstone	C R C R
Black Turnstone	C U C C
Surfbird	C U C C
Red Knot	C R U R
Sanderling	C C C C
Semipalmated Sandpiper	X R R -
Western Sandpiper	C C C U
Least Sandpiper	C C C U
Baird's Sandpiper	R R U -
Pectoral Sandpiper	R X C -
Sharp-tailed Sandpiper	X - R -
Rock Sandpiper(L)	U - U U
Dunlin	C R C C
Stilt Sandpiper	- X X -
Buff-breasted Sandpiper(L)	- X R -
Ruff	- - R -
Short-billed Dowitcher	C C C X
Long-billed Dowitcher	C R C U
Common Snipe	C U C C
Wilson's Phalarope	X - X -
Red-necked Phalarope	C U C -
Red Phalarope(P)	U R U R
South Polar Skua(P)	- R U -
Pomarine Jaeger(P)	C U C R
Parasitic Jaeger	C R C -
Long-tailed Jaeger(P)	X X U -
Franklin's Gull	X - R -
Bonaparte's Gull	U R U U
Heermann's Gull	R C C R
Mew Gull	C R C C
Ring-billed Gull	C C C C
California Gull	U U C U
Herring Gull	U - U U
Thayer's Gull	R - R R
Western Gull	C C C C
Glaucous-winged Gull	C C C C
Glaucous Gull	R X - R

Species	Season S S F W
Black-legged Kittiwake	U U U U
Red-legged Kittiwake(P)	X X X X
Sabine's Gull(P)	C U C -
Caspian Tern	C C C X
Elegant Tern(I)	- R R -
Common Tern	U R C -
Arctic Tern(P)	U R C -
Black Tern	- - X -
Common Murre	C C C C
Thick-billed Murre(P)	- - X X
Pigeon Guillemot	C C C U
Marbled Murrelet	U U U U
Xantus's Murrelet(P)	X X R X
Ancient Murrelet(P)	X X X R
Cassin's Auklet(P)	C U C U
Parakeet Auklet(P)	X - - X
Rhinoceros Auklet	C C C U
Tufted Puffin(L)	U U U R
Horned Puffin(P)	X X X X
Rock Dove	C C C C
Band-tailed Pigeon	U U U R
Mourning Dove	U U U R
Barn Owl	C C C C
Western Screech-Owl	C C C C
Great Horned Owl	C C C C
Snowy Owl(I)	R - R R
Northern Pygmy-Owl	U U U U
Spotted Owl(L)	R R R R
Barred Owl	R R R R
Long-eared Owl	X - X X
Short-eared Owl	U R U U
Northern Saw-whet Owl	U U U U
Common Nighthawk	- U R -
Black Swift	R U U -
Vaux's Swift	C C C -
Anna's Hummingbird	X - - R
Rufous Hummingbird	C C U -
Belted Kingfisher	C C C C
Red-breasted Sapsucker	U U U U
Downy Woodpecker	C C C C
Hairy Woodpecker	C C C C
Northern Flicker	C C C C
Pileated Woodpecker	U U U U
Olive-sided Flycatcher	U C U -
Western Wood-Pewee	U U U -
Willow Flycatcher	R C C -
Hammond's Flycatcher	C C C -
Pacific-slope Flycatcher	C C C -
Tropical Kingbird	- - R X

Species	Season S S F W
Western Kingbird	R X R -
Eastern Kingbird	- X X -
Northern Shrike	U - U U
Cassin's Vireo	U U U -
Hutton's Vireo	C C C C
Warbling Vireo	C C C -
Red-eyed Vireo(L)	- R R -
Gray Jay(L)	C C C C
Steller's Jay	C C C C
Western Scrub-Jay	U U U U
American Crow	C C C C
Northwestern Crow(L-North)	U U U U
Common Raven	C C C C
Horned Lark(L)	U U U U
Purple Martin(L)	R R R -
Tree Swallow	C C C -
Violet-green Swallow	C C C -
N. Rough-winged Swallow	U U U -
Bank Swallow	X X R -
Barn Swallow	C C C -
Cliff Swallow	C C C -
Black-capped Chickadee	C C C C
Mountain Chickadee	X X X X
Chestnut-backed Chickadee	C C C C
Bushtit	U U U U
Red-breasted Nuthatch(I)	U U U U
Brown Creeper	U U U U
Bewick's Wren	C C C C
House Wren(L)	U U U -
Winter Wren	C C C C
Marsh Wren	C C C C
American Dipper(L)	U U U U
Golden-crowned Kinglet	C C C C
Ruby-crowned Kinglet	C R C C
Western Bluebird	R X R X
Mountain Bluebird	R X R X
Townsend's Solitaire	U U R R
Swainson's Thrush	C C C -
Hermit Thrush	R U U R
American Robin	C C C C
Varied Thrush	C C C C
European Starling	C C C C
Northern Mockingbird	X - X X

Species	Season S S F W
American Pipit	C X C R
Cedar Waxwing	U C C U
Orange-crowned Warbler	C C C R
Yellow Warbler	C C C X
Yellow-rumped Warbler-	
Myrtle	C - C C
Audubon	C C C U
Black-throated Gray Warbler	C C C X
Townsend's Warbler	C U C U
Hermit Warbler(L)	U U U -
Palm Warbler(L)	X - R R
MacGillivray's Warbler	C C U -
Common Yellowthroat	C C C R
Wilson's Warbler	C C C -
Western Tanager	C C C -
Spotted Towhee	C C C C
Chipping Sparrow(L)	U U R -
Vesper Sparrow	X X X -
Savannah Sparrow	C C C R
Fox Sparrow	C U C C
Song Sparrow	C C C C
Lincoln's Sparrow	U - U R

Species	Season S S F W
Swamp Sparrow	- - X X
White-throated Sparrow	R - R R
White-crowned Sparrow	C C C X
Golden-crowned Sparrow	C - C C
Dark-eyed Junco	C C C C
Lapland Longspur	R - U R
Snow Bunting	R - R R
Black-headed Grosbeak	C C C -
Red-winged Blackbird	C C C C
Western Meadowlark	U R U U
Yellow-headed Blackbird	X X X -
Brewer's Blackbird	C C C C
Brown-headed Cowbird	C C U R
Bullock's Oriole(L)	U U - X
Pine Grosbeak(L)	R R R R
Purple Finch	C C C C
House Finch	C C C C
Red Crossbill(I)	U U U U
Pine Siskin(I)	C C C C
American Goldfinch	C C C U
Evening Grosbeak	C U U U
House Sparrow	U U U U

The following species have been recorded less than 5 times or are now extirpated in the area (E):

Short-tailed Albatross(P)
Shy Albatross(P)
Cook's Petrel(P)
Wedge-tailed Shearwater (P)
Wilson's Storm-Petrel(P)
Red-billed Tropicbird(P)
American White Pelican
Magnificent Frigatebird
White Ibis
White-faced Ibis
Ross's Goose
Mute Swan
Falcated Duck
Garganey
King Eider
Red-shouldered Hawk
Swainson's Hawk
Ferruginous Hawk
Prairie Falcon
Mountain Plover
Eurasian Dotterel
Gray-tailed Tattler
Upland Sandpiper
Great Knot
Curlew Sandpiper
Laughing Gull
Little Gull

Black-headed Gull
Iceland Gull
Ivory Gull
Least Tern
White-winged Dove
Yellow-billed Cuckoo(E)
Burrowing Owl(E)
Calliope Hummingbird
Lewis's Woodpecker(E)
Red-naped Sapsucker
Eastern Phoebe
Say's Phoebe
Ash-throated Flycatcher
Scissor-tailed Flycatcher
Fork-tailed Flycatcher
Blue Jay
Clark's Nutcracker
Black-billed Magpie
White-breasted Nuthatch
Pygmy Nuthatch
Blue-gray Gnatcatcher
Sage Thrasher
Yellow Wagtail
White Wagtail
Black-backed Wagtail
Bohemian Waxwing
Tennessee Warbler
Nashville Warbler
Northern Parula
Magnolia Warbler
Black-throated Blue Warbler

Blackburnian Warbler
Blackpoll Warbler
Black-and-White Warbler
American Redstart
Northern Waterthrush
American Tree Sparrow
Clay-colored Sparrow
Lark Sparrow
Black-throated Sparrow
Lark Bunting
LeConte's Sparrow
Harris's Sparrow
Chestnut-collared Longspur
McKay's Bunting
Lazuli Bunting
Dickcissel
Bobolink
Rusty Blackbird
Hooded Oriole
Brambling
Gray-crowned Rosy-Finch
White-winged Crossbill

This checklist was compiled through the efforts of Glen and Wanda Hoge, Gene Hunn, Phil Mattocks, Steve Mlodinow, Bob Morse, Russell Rogers, Fred Sharpe, and Bill Tweit.
07/01

WASHINGTON COASTAL SPECIALTIES

Birders coming to the Washington coast often target certain birds for their visit. These birds are considered the Specialties of the Washington coast. The 82 Coastal Specialties are identified below with information on when and where they may be found as well as key identification criteria on some species. Color photographs are included for most of these species.

Red-throated Loon

Red-throated Loon   Jim Pruske

A common winter through spring visitor to the open bays of the Grays Harbor, Willapa, and Columbia River estuaries. Summers in small numbers around the partially submerged rocks at the far east end of the Ocean Shores jetty where it meets the shore at the game range near the Snowy Plover nesting area. Try for this species at Clallam Bay, the end of Damon Point, the west end of the Ocean Shores jetty, the Westport jetty, and the Ilwaco boat basin.

Pacific Loon

Pacific Loon   James R. Gallagher/Sea and Sage Audubon

Common spring and fall migrant, uncommon in winter. Check Clallam Bay, the end of Damon Point, and loons passing by the Ocean Shores jetty, Westport jetty, and the North jetty of the Columbia River.

Yellow-billed Loon

Yellow-billed Loon   Ruth Sullivan

Rare winter visitor; reported almost annually. Most records are from Neah Bay, Ocean Shores, and Westport. Many are immature birds where bill shape is not as evident as adults but plumage marks and bill color clearly identifies them as a Yellow-billed Loon. Several recent summer and early fall records near Grays Harbor suggest that one should be on the lookout for this species during these seasons as well.

Black-footed Albatross

Black-footed Albatross   Jeff Skriletz

Common pelagic species seen on most of the Westport Seabirds boat trips out of Westport.

Laysan Albatross

Laysan Albatross   Terence Wahl

Uncommon pelagic species most often seen November through April in the deep water at Grays Canyon.

Northern Fulmar

Northern Fulmar   Terry Sisson

Common pelagic species seen on most Westport boat trips. They are occasionally seen from shore during or after fall/winter storms. Dark morph plumages predominate.

Pink-footed Shearwater

Pink-footed Shearwater   Olympic National Park

Common summer and fall pelagic species. Very rarely seen from shore.

Flesh-footed Shearwater

Flesh-footed Shearwater   Terence Wahl

Uncommon pelagic species found on about ½ of the trips between May and November; October records predominate. Most often seen among the large numbers of Sooty Shearwaters concentrated around shrimp trawlers.

Buller's Shearwater

Buller's Shearwater   Terence Wahl

Common pelagic species mid August through October. Very rarely observed from shore.

Sooty Shearwater

Sooty Shearwater   James R. Gallagher/Sea and Sage Audubon

One of the few pelagic species consistently seen from shore. Look for the long lines of Sooty Shearwaters migrating along the coast from July to October (best in early fall) with their rapid wing beats followed by a glide. Good spots to watch for migrating Sooty Shearwaters are the Ocean Shores jetty, Westport jetty, the North jetty of the Columbia River, and the North Head Lighthouse.

Short-tailed Shearwater

Short-tailed Shearwater   Terence Wahl

An uncommon September and October and mid winter pelagic species. Occasionally seen from shore.

Fork-tailed Storm-Petrel

Fork-tailed Storm-Petrel   Terence Wahl

Common May through October pelagic species. Strong on-shore winds can produce sightings from the Ocean Shores jetty.

Leach's Storm-Petrel

Uncommon pelagic species most often seen in July and August or over deep water in April. Nests on Destruction Island and Quillayute Needles. During the breeding season, storm-petrels are nocturnal leaving their nests and returning under cover of darkness.

Brown Pelican

Brown Pelican   Terry Sisson

Common mid May through early November as a visitor from Southern California, Baja, and the Sea of Cortez. Easily seen in Long Beach, Columbia River estuary, Westport, Ocean Shores, and occasionally along the North Coast. Seems to be increasing in numbers and length of stay in Washington.

Brandt's Cormorant

Brandt's Cormorant   James R. Gallagher/Sea and Sage Audubon

Uncommon spring through fall cormorant on rock outcrops, jetties, and nearby waters. Nests on open grassy tops of offshore islands along the North Coast and on the cliffs at Cape Disappointment. Check the ledges below the Cape Disappointment Lighthouse, the far end of the Ocean Shores jetty, and watch for Brandt's Cormorants passing by the Ocean Shores jetty and the North Jetty.

Pelagic Cormorant

Pelagic Cormorant   Dennis Paulson

Common resident along the coast. Nests among the rock cliffs of the North Coast including Cape Flattery and Pt. Grenville. Also nests at Cape Disappointment. Check any of the coastal jetties, nearby waters, and pilings at marinas.

Emperor Goose

Emperor Goose   Keith Brady

Less than annual winter visitor; sometimes with Canada Geese and Brant flocks in coastal pastures and sometimes found alone on beaches. Records come from Neah Bay, La Push, Ocean Shores, Tokeland, the Palix River, and the Long Beach Peninsula.

Canada Goose (forms)

There are 8 subspecies of Canada Goose found along the coast with six identifiable groups. From the largest to smallest, they are:

1. <u>Giant Canada Goose</u> (*Branta canadenis maxima*) A huge goose, which may have a white spot on the forehead and a chin strap with a hook-like extension. A small introduced population resides near the mouth of the Columbia River.

2. <u>Western Canada Goose</u> (*B. c. moffitti*) Our most common Canada Goose. A large goose and the only one which regularly breeds along the coast. Breast colors range from light gray in young birds to almost white in adults. Originally a migratory species, this goose has become a year round resident at a number of coastal locations.

3. <u>Vancouver Canada Goose</u> (*B. c. fulva*) and <u>Dusky Canada Goose</u> (*B. c. occidentalis*) Medium to large geese with a dark brown breast which mergers into the black neck. Almost the size of the Western. Winters in the Willapa National Wildlife Refuge and in the lower Columbia River. The Dusky Canada Goose is "threatened" as defined by the Endangered Species Act

4. <u>Lesser Canada Goose</u> (*B. c. parvipes*) and <u>Taverner's Canada Goose</u> (*B. c. taverneri*) Medium sized geese with a gray to nearly white breast. Winters in small numbers along the Columbia River. Can have a white neck ring but almost always incomplete. Wary, flies high in large flocks typically of more than 200 birds.

5. <u>Aleutian Canada Goose</u> (*B. c. leucopareia*) A small species of Canada Goose with a dark grayish brown breast. Has broad white ring between the neck and the breast with a black band below the ring. A few migrate along the coast; most winter in northern California. Not all individuals are separable in the field

from Cackling Canada Goose.

6. <u>Cackling Canada Goose</u> (*B. c. minima*) The smallest Canada Goose; 1½ times the size of a Mallard. Short neck, dark breast that may have a purplish cast, and short, stubby bill. Some have white neck rings, normally thin and incomplete. Check the Willapa NWR for this subspecies.

Cackling Canada Goose   Jim Pruske

Two of the better places to study the different Canada Goose subspecies are the Riekkola Unit of the Willapa NWR and the farmlands south of Raymond.

Brant

Brant   Jeff Skriletz

Common spring and uncommon fall and winter goose of the bay of Grays Harbor. Common winter visitor to the Willapa National Wildlife Refuge and the west side of Long Island where it feeds on eelgrass. A few often summer along the coast.

Trumpeter Swan

Uncommon spring and fall migrant and winter visitor in the freshwater ponds and lakes along the coast. In winter, check Lake Quinault, the ponds at Ocean City State Park, Black Lake in Seaview, the Fort Canby State Park ponds, and Ilwaco.

Trumpeter Swan   Terry Sisson

Eurasian Wigeon

Eurasian Wigeon   James R. Gallagher/Sea and Sage Audubon

Uncommon wigeon seen in large flocks of wintering American Wigeons often in ratios of 1:200. During the hunting season, check the Satsop Development Park pond. In winter, check the Brady Loop Road, Wenzel Slough Road, the flooded fields south of South Bend, south of the Palix River, and the large American Wigeon flocks on Willapa Bay, especially near the Bruceville–Bruceport Heritage Marker.

Harlequin Duck

Harlequin Duck   Keith Brady

The only duck in North America that breeds in steep mountain streams. Nests in the Quinault River along the Enchanted Valley Trail from Graves Creek to Enchanted Valley. Winters in small numbers along the strait and coast. In winter, try Clallam Bay, Makah Bay, La Push, and the east end of the Westport Jetty. In spring and summer, try the Quinault River from the end of the paved South Shore Road to Graves Creek and up the Enchanted Valley Trail.

Black Scoter

Uncommon fall through spring scoter in the salt water bays along the coast. Check Neah Bay, the bay at the east end of the Ocean Shores jetty, and the east end of the Westport jetty. A few sometimes summer in Ocean Shores.

White-tailed Kite

White-tailed Kite   Peter Knapp

Rare local resident of open farmlands along the South Coast. Year round search the top of conifers along the Elk Prairie Road east of LeBam, Julia Butler Hansen Refuge, the Chinook Valley Road, and Puget Island. In fall and winter, check Leadbetter Point.

Peregrine Falcon

Uncommon, fast flying raptor of the coast. Nests along the North Coast between Cape Flattery and Pt. Grenville. Look for them on James Island, at Second Beach near La Push, Pt. Grenville and on other North Coast cliffs. Widespread during migration and winter where shorebirds occur. Most often seen from late September through May. Regularly hunts the Ocean Shores Game Range. Can be seen at Bowerman Basin during spring migration

Peregrine Falcon   Team Caven

where it hunts the shorebirds on the mud flats. Most are the coastal subspecies, *pealei*.

Gyrfalcon

Rare in winter. Most reports come from Ocean Shores but also rarely from the Brady Loop Road.

Blue Grouse

Common nester in higher elevations of the coniferous and mixed woodlands on the North Coast and uncommon down to sea level. Reliable spots to see and hear this bird from mid April through June are the Willoughby Ridge Road, the upper end of the Quinault Ridge Road, and the upper end of the upper Wynoochee Valley.

Blue Grouse   Jim Pruske

Mountain Quail

Mountain Quail   James R. Gallagher/Sea and Sage Audubon

Rare resident of the clear cuts in the Satsop River drainage and along the Cloquallum Road northeast of Elma. In April and May, search for calling Mountain Quail at dawn in clear cuts north of Brady and Elma.

American Golden-Plover

American Golden-Plover, adult   James R. Gallagher/Sea and Sage Audubon

American Golden-Plover, juvenile   Dennis Paulson

Uncommon August through October migrant on the sandy beaches, sparsely vegetated dunes, mudflats, and *Salicornia* marshes of Grays Harbor and Leadbetter Point. Peak of fall migration is from mid September through mid October. A very few come through as spring migrants from early April to mid May. The best places to look are on the sand spit at the Ocean Shores Game Range, Bill's Spit, and the *Salicornia* marsh behind the Sewage Treatment Plant in Ocean Shores, Bottle Beach, and Leadbetter Point. Spring and fall flocks can include both species of golden-plover and separation of golden-plovers can be very difficult. Criteria for immatures and basic adults include primary wing extension (but beware of effects of molt), structure, and voice. (see references listed under Pacific Golden-Plover).

Pacific Golden-Plover

Pacific Golden-Polver, adult   James R. Gallagher/Sea and Sage Audubon

Pacific Golden-Polver, juvenile   Dennis Paulson

Uncommon fall migrant (with peak numbers between mid August through mid October). Adults migrate through as early as late June, with juveniles arriving in late August or early September. Most Pacific Golden-Plover leave by late October. Spring migration, in fewer numbers, occurs from early April to mid May. They prefer similar habitat as the American Golden-Plover. Both species of golden-plover may be on the Ocean Shores golf course during storms and heavy winds. Some richly colored immatures can be easily identified by their buffy-orange underparts, but duller individuals are problematic. See Paulson (1993), Mlodinow and O'Brien (1996), and Mlodinow (1993) for further identification information.

Snowy Plover

Snowy Plover   Ruth Sullivan

Endangered nester from mid March through late August at Midway Beach (Grayland), Leadbetter Point, and perhaps a few still nest at Ocean Shores. The best places to search are where the Midway Beach Road reaches the beach (in the appropriate upper beach habitat), the Warrenton Cannery Road where it meets the beach, and the west side of the Leadbetter Point peninsula south of the designated nesting area. Please do not enter any designated Snowy Plover Nesting area.

Black Oystercatcher

Black Oystercatcher   Ruth Sullivan

Uncommon resident of the rocky outcroppings along the North Coast. They feed on shellfish and crustaceans on exposed rocks of the intertidal zone. Best spots are the rocks below the south side overlook at Pt. Grenville, the rocks below Cape Flattery, the rocky spots between Sekiu and Neah Bay, the base of the jetty at the west end of Neah Bay, Rialto Beach, Copalis Rock, and the rocks below the North Head Lighthouse.

Willet

Willet   Ruth Sullivan

Uncommon long-legged shorebird seen from fall through spring along the South Coast. In fall and winter, the best spots to check are the rock breakwater beyond the marina in Tokeland at high tide, Graveyard Spit, and the end of Emerson Avenue in Tokeland.

Wandering Tattler

Wandering Tattler   Ruth Sullivan

A common shorebird of the Ocean Shores jetty, Westport jetty, and the North jetty of the Columbia River. Seen from mid April through May, late July through mid October. Usually one can be found by walking along the Ocean Shores jetty toward the end.

Whimbrel

Whimbrel   Jim Pruske

Common spring and fall migrant to the mudflats around Grays Harbor and Long Beach Peninsula. Some are present all summer and a few may even winter. Check the Ocean Shores Game Range, Bill's Spit, Bottle Beach, and Leadbetter Point (one to two hours before or after high tide).

Long-billed Curlew

Long-billed Curlew   Ruth Sullivan

Winters along the South Coast especially in Tokeland. A few are present year round. Check the rock breakwater off the Tokeland marina at high tide or Graveyard Spit during other tides.

Bar-tailed Godwit

Bar-tailed Godwit, juvenile   Ruth Sullivan

The best places for this rare Asiatic shorebird are the rock breakwater and the marina in Tokeland at high tide and Bill's Spit in Ocean Shores (1 – 2 hours before and after high tide). Most records are from mid August through mid October with a peak in September. Usually the Bar-tailed Godwit is among a flock of Marbled Godwit and sometimes easy to pick out by the pale gray underparts of the adult versus the buff colors of the fall Marbled Godwit but beware of pale Marbled Godwits. See Paulson (1993) for further identification information.

Marbled Godwit

Marbled Godwit   James R. Gallagher/Sea and Sage Audubon

Common migrant from April through early May and from July to October along the South Coast and uncommon winter resident at Tokeland. In Ocean Shores, check Bill's Spit and the game range; Bottle Beach, and Leadbetter Point – all 1 or 2 hours before or after high tide.

Ruddy Turnstone

Ruddy Turnstone   Jeff Skriletz

Common spring and less common fall migrant along the entire coast. Their preferred habitat is mudflats and beaches with cobbled rocks although they are often seen with Black Turnstone and Surfbird on rock jetties and Sanderling, Red Knot, and Dunlin on open beaches. One of the better places has been among the cobbled rocks along the beach on the upper west side of the Leadbetter Point peninsula.

Black Turnstone

Black Turnstone   Keith Brady

Common rock shorebird along the entire coast from mid July through May. Feeds on small limpets, barnacles, and other crustaceans. At high tide, look for them at the end of Emerson Avenue in Tokeland, on the Ocean Shores, Westport, and North jetties, and rock outcrops along the North Coast including the rocks at Ruby Beach and Neah Bay.

Surfbird

Surfbird   Patrick Sullivan

Common rock shorebird along the entire coast and the western Strait of Juan de Fuca from late July through April. Prefers rock jetties and rock outcrops. Check the three jetties of the South Coast, the rocks at Ruby Beach, the rocks between the mouth of the Sekiu River and Neah Bay, and the rocks below the North Head Lighthouse.

Baird's Sandpiper

Baird's Sandpiper   Ruth Sullivan

Uncommon fall migrant (early August to early October) often found feeding on insects along dry, sandy upper beaches. Try the north side of the Damon Point Road at low tide and the Ocean Shores Game Range. Very rare in spring and summer.

Sharp-tailed Sandpiper

Sharp-tailed Sandpiper, juvenile   Ruth Sullivan

Rare Asiatic shorebird on the South Coast from late September to late October. Most often found among small flocks of Pectoral Sandpipers in the *Salicornia* marsh at the Ocean Shores Game Range and to the west of Grassy Isle at Leadbetter Point. Virtually all observations are of juvenile birds.

Rock Sandpiper

Rock Sandpiper, right; Surfbird, left   Patrick Sullivan

Uncommon winter visitor to the rock jetties and outcrops along the coast appearing early October and leaving mid April. Diminishing in numbers along the South Coast. Best chances are the Ocean Shores and Westport jetties where a few winter. In Ocean Shores, they are often at the base of the jetty at high tide. In strong west winds, the Westport jetty birds may seek refuge among the rock groins near the observation platform in Westport or on the breakwater wall to the east of the marina.

Buff-breasted Sandpiper

Buff-breasted Sandpiper   Ruth Sullivan

A rare shorebird that often shows up in late August and early September around the sparsely vegetated edges of the Damon Point Pond or Leadbetter Point.

Red Phalarope

Red Phalarope   Ruth Sullivan

A pelagic shorebird of the open ocean seen on boat trips from April to May and July through October with the highest numbers viewed from late August to early September. May seek protection in small ponds and bays along the coast during November and December storms.

South Polar Skua

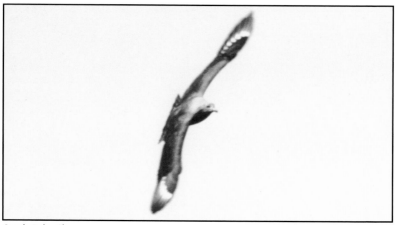

South Polar Skua   Terence Wahl

Uncommon pelagic species from mid August through October. Seen on over 90% of the trips in September and October and half of the trips in July and August.

Pomarine Jaeger

Pomarine Jaeger   Ned Harris

Common pelagic species seen in mid May and from mid July through September. Occasionally seen from shore.

Parasitic Jaeger

Parasitic Jaeger   Terence Wahl

Common pelagic species seen in May and from mid August through October. Regularly seen from the jetties in fall chasing terns. Spring numbers are variable onshore.

Long-tailed Jaeger

Long-tailed Jaeger   Keith Brady

Uncommon pelagic species seen from August through early September. Very rarely seen from shore.

Heermann's Gull

Heermann's Gull   Jim Pruske

Common in July to October along the outer coast and the western Strait of Juan de Fuca. A few show up in June and November and occasionally stay into winter.

Mew Gull

Mew Gull   James R. Gallagher/Sea and Sage Audubon

Common from September to May among the open pastures of the South Coast, in tide rips on saltwater, and in roosting flocks on the beaches. Begin to appear on the North Coast (Clallam Bay) in mid July and the South Coast by late August. In winter, check the Raymond Water Treatment Plant, the flooded fields south of South Bend, the fields just south of the Palix River, and other open beaches and fields along the South Coast.

Thayer's Gull

Thayer's Gull, adult — Terence Wahl

Thayer's Gull, first winter — James R. Gallagher/Sea and Sage Audubon

Uncommon to rare fall to spring visitor to the open beaches of the coast. It is less common than the Herring Gull along the outer coast. In winter, check Neah Bay, La Push, Taholah, Ocean Shores, and Westport. Immatures predominate. The separation of the immature Thayer's Gull from the Glaucous-winged X Western Gull is the very difficult for novices at gull identification. The separation of adults is less difficult but still tough. Size and structure are the key marks. Zimmer (1985) offers an excellent summary of Thayer's Gull identification.

Western Gull

Western Gull   Ruth Sullivan

This common gull along the coast hybridizes extensively with Glaucous-winged Gulls so that many of the large gulls along the coast are Western X Glaucous-winged hybrid gulls. The interbreeding sometimes makes it difficult to identify a "pure" Western Gull. In fall and winter identification of adults, look for the Western's dark mantle, no or minimal head streaking, and yellow orbital ring. Most of the Western Gulls reside along the outer coast.

Glaucous-winged Gull

Glaucous-winged Gull   Terry Sisson

This large, common gull along the coast and further inland has a pale gray mantle and wings versus the darker mantle and wings of the Western Gull. The most common large gull away from the coast.

Glaucous Gull

Glaucous Gull   Terence Wahl

Uncommon to rare winter and early spring visitor to the coast and Straits of Juan de Fuca. Many of the Glaucous Gulls are first winter birds with a very pale (almost white) mantle and wings and a bicolored bill. Beware of faded young Glaucous-winged Gulls, April to June. Generally larger than either the Western or Glaucous-winged Gulls. In winter, check the mouth of the Sekiu River, La Push, and near the seafood processing plants in Westport.

Black-legged Kittiwake

Black-legged Kittiwake   Terence Wahl

Common September through mid April on pelagic trips. Onshore, seen spring and fall in La Push, the channel between Ocean Shores and Westport, on the pilings off the Coast Guard Station in Westport, and the Columbia River mouth. Non-breeding birds are also present some summer in the same areas.

Sabine's Gull

Sabine's Gull   Terence Wahl

Common pelagic species especially in May, August, and September but seen most of the remainder of the year on boat trips out of Westport. Very rarely seen from shore.

Elegant Tern

Elegant Tern   James R. Gallagher/Sea and Sage Audubon

Rare wanderer from California to the open beaches of the coast largely during El Nino years. Reported from Columbia River mouth, Willapa and Grays Harbor bays, Ocean Shores, and more rarely on the North Coast.

Arctic Tern

Arctic Tern   James R. Gallagher/Sea and Sage Audubon

Uncommon May and July through September pelagic migrant. May be sometimes seen from shore.

Caspian Tern

Caspian Tern   Jeff Skriletz

Common, raucous tern along the coast from March through September, with a few lingering into November in Tokeland. Often heard calling before being seen.

Common Murre

Common Murre   Terry Sisson

Uncommon nester on the rock cliffs of the North Coast with the largest colony at Tatoosh Island. Can be observed anywhere along the outer coast from late July through the end of August. Juveniles are often present resulting in mis-identification as murrelets.

Pigeon Guillemot

Pigeon Guillemot   Dennis Paulson

Common nester in rock jetties, cliff crevices, and among the rubble of rocks and driftwood along the North Coast and the Strait of Juan de Fuca. Can be seen at Clallam Bay, Neah Bay, Cape Flattery, La Push, Pt. Grenville, and from the jetties on the South Coast.

Marbled Murrelet

Marbled Murrelet   Ruth Sullivan

Marbled Murrelets do not build nests but lay single eggs on large, often moss covered, tree limbs in the upper canopy of large old-growth trees of the Olympic Mountains and the Willapa Hills. Daily, they fly up to 50 to 60 miles inland from marine waters to bring fish to a single chick. Before dawn, they may be seen or heard returning to the nesting area during breeding season (late April through July; but height of activity is the first three weeks of July). Best locations are at the Campbell Tree Grove campground, Quinault Rain Forest Nature Trail, Quinault Natural Recreational Trail, along the upper parts of the Willoughby Ridge Road, or on Long Island. They fly at a speed of 45 to 85 miles per hour with rapid wingbeats. Best chance for seeing this species is to quietly watch for a dark, rapidly moving bird against a light sky in the predawn hours and up to an hour after dawn on mornings with high overcast clouds. Listen for their diagnostic "Keeer" call (somewhat like a Northern Flicker or a distant gull call). After nesting, spends the remainder of the year on the salt water. Declining in abundance primarily due to loss of forest habitat, this species is found on the water more frequently on the North Coast. Search just offshore of the kelp line at Clallam Bay, mouth of the Sekiu River, Neah Bay, and La Push. In Ocean Shores, look at the east-end of Damon Point and off the tip of the jetty. To assist the Washington State Department of Fish and Wildlife track Marbled Murrelets, birders are encouraged to report evidence of nests or observations of murrelets flying beneath tree tops to Eric Cummins, Wildlife Management Program, Dept. of Fish & Wildlife, 600 Capitol Way, Olympia, WA, 98501.

Long-billed Murrelet

Long-billed Murrelet   Robert Howson

Rare Asiatic vagrant to the Washington coast. Two seen on August 4, 1999 on the south side of Damon Point. See Mlodinow (1997) for further identification information.

Ancient Murrelet

Uncommon winter pelagic species. Sometimes seen from shore at Sekiu and Neah Bay.

Cassin's Auklet

A uncommon burrow nester on the offshore islands of the North Coast including Tatoosh, Bodelteh, and Destruction Islands. Declining in numbers in recent years. Common on pelagic trips in April and late September through October. Uncommon on pelagic trips in summer and winter.

Rhinoceros Auklet

Rhinoceros Auklet   Jim Pruske

Nests in burrows among open grassy hillsides on offshore islands including Destruction and Tatoosh. Commonly seen in summer from the South coast jetties, Clallam Bay, and Cape Flattery where it nests.

Tufted Puffin

Tufted Puffin   Olympic Coast National Marine Sanctuary

Uncommon and declining burrow nester in the grassy hillsides of the offshore islands and seen irregularly on pelagic trips. Best chances are to search for this species during the breeding season (May through early August) at Cape Flattery, Kohchaa Island (La Push), and the furthest island south of Pt. Grenville. Contact Puffin Adventures (1-888-305-2437) in Neah Bay for boat trips to see the Tufted Puffin around Tatoosh Island and Cape Flattery.

Snowy Owl

Snowy Owl   Ruth Sullivan

Rare fall and winter migrant along the coast. In invasion years, they most often appear at Ocean Shores (normally on Damon Point or the game range), Leadbetter Point, and Waatch River mouth. Check the Bird Box or Tweeters for recent reports.

Spotted Owl

Spotted Owl   Ruth Sullivan

This threatened species resides in the old growth forest of the Olympic Mountains, It prefers steep hillsides with nearby water. The best chance to see or hear this bird is along the Third Beach Trail (La Push), the east end of Lake Quinault on the Colonel Bob Trail, or in that general area. The Spotted Owl calls mostly in the months of April through July, most frequently pre-dawn and after dusk. It is important to realize that this species is threatened with extinction and already subjected to legitimate studies to aid their conservation. Please be judicious of any intrusion into their territory.

Black Swift

The status of Black Swift along the North Coast is uncertain. There have been sightings from Cape Flattery and other rocky coast locations suggesting that this species may nest in the sea cliffs along the coast. Most sightings are from early morning, dusk, or during overcast days. To gain a better understanding of the Black Swift status, please report any sightings to a Regional Editor of *North American Birds* (See Coastal Birding Organizations Appendix).

Tropical Kingbird

Tropical Kingbird   Ruth Sullivan

A small number of immature birds disperse north along the West Coast of the United States sometimes reaching the coast of Washington from early October through late November. There is no specific place to see this species along the coast; just look and listen for Tropical Kingbirds on exposed perches such as telephone wires, fences, and trees. Check the Bird Box and Tweeters for recent reports.

Hutton's Vireo

Hutton's Vireo   James R. Gallagher/Sea and Sage Audubon

Uncommon resident of the coniferous woodlands (particularly second growth) along the entire coast. Most easily found when vocal. Singing is most frequent from February through May.

Northwestern Crow

Northwestern Crow   Bob Morse

Common crow of the North Coast where it scavenges along the shore. Easily seen at LaPush and Neah Bay. Voice is somewhat lower and hoarser than American Crow. Controversy about the degree of genetic separation from the American Crow at the southern edge of the Northwestern Crow's range is considerable and criteria for field identification are uncertain.

American Pipit

American Pipit   Ruth Sullivan

Common migrant in April, May, September and October in sparsely vegetated habitats. Check the Game Range at Ocean Shores, Damon Point, Leadbetter Point, and the Waatch River mouth.

Townsend's Warbler

Townsend's Warbler   James R. Gallagher/Sea and Sage Audubon

Uncommon winter visitor to the Sitka spruce forests along the outer coast. Check Sitka spruce woods at Ocean Shores, Westport, North Head, and Long Beach Peninsula. A scare breeder in the higher elevation coniferous forests on the west slope of the Olympic Mountains but beware of the relatively frequent hybridization with Hermit Warbler. Try the Quinault Ridge Road in fall.

Palm Warbler

Palm Warbler   Patrick Sullivan

Rare fall migrant and winter visitor to scrubby habitats on the outer coast. The most consistent locations have been the Scotch Broom in Tokeland and in Ocean Shores at the intersection of Point Brown Avenue and Marine View Drive, and between the marina and the retirement home along Catala Avenue

Fox Sparrow

"Sooty" Fox Sparrow (*unalaschcensis*)   Ruth Sullivan

Common from mid September through mid May in brush and thickets along the coast.

The Fox Sparrow may be split into four species. The *unalaschcensis* group of the Fox Sparrow may become the Sooty Fox Sparrow. This uniform dark plumaged sparrow breeds rarely and winters commonly in the undergrowth of coniferous and mixed woodlands along the coast.

The other two species found in Washington would be the Red Fox Sparrow and the Slate-colored Sparrow. They are accidental to coastal Washington.

Further information of this matter is provided in Zink and Kessen's (1999).

Golden-crowned Sparrow

Golden-crowned Sparrow   Jim Pruske

Common winter resident from mid September through mid May in brush and thickets along the coast. Try Friend's Landing, along the Sandridge Road and the Chinook Valley Road east of Ilwaco.

Lapland Longspur

Lapland Longspur   Ruth Sullivan

Uncommon mid September to mid November migrant to the sparsely vegetated habitat of Leadbetter Point, Ocean Shores Game

Range, Damon Point, and between the Sewer Treatment Plant fence and the jetty rocks in Ocean Shores.

Red Crossbill

Red Crossbill   James R. Gallagher/Sea and Sage Audubon

There are at least 9 distinct types of Red Crossbill in the United States of which 3 may be seen along the Washington coast. The key differences between the types are based on bill profile, vocalization, and preference of seed crop. The following Red Crossbill types are found along the coast:

Type 1 These crossbills are associated with Sitka spruce and western hemlock seeds. Check the Sitka spruce trees along the Second Beach and Slough trails near La Push for this type.

Type 3 These small crossbills are associated with western hemlock and spruce seeds. Check the western hemlock trees along the Willoughby Ridge Road and along the road to the Campbell Tree Grove for this type.

Type 4 These crossbills are associated with Douglas fir seeds. Douglas fir trees are prevalent along the coast so this type may occur anywhere in that habitat.

More information of the different Red Crossbill types is provided in Sibley (2000) and DeBenedictis (1995) and web site http://research.amnh.org/ornithology/crossbills/.

COASTAL BIRDING ORGANIZATIONS

The local, mid-coast Audubon chapter is the **Grays Harbor Audubon Society**. Their mailing address is P. O. Box 444, Montesano, **WA**, 98563 and their web address is http://www.audubon.org/chapter/wa/ghas. This Audubon chapter meets monthly, produces a monthly newsletter, the *Sandpiper*, and is involved with the a number of significant local environmental issues including the acquisition and protection of tracts of sensitive land in the Grays Harbor area.

The **Grays Harbor Bird Club**, a long-time local birding club, is interested in birding. More information about their field trips and meetings may be obtained by contacting Rose DuBois at 360-532-4067.

The **Willapa Hills Audubon Society**, located in Longview, covers the area along the Columbia River west to and including the Long Beach Peninsula. This 300 member conservation and education based Audubon chapter has monthly meetings and field trips. For more information and a complimentary newsletter, contact President Kay Beck, Willapa Hills Audubon Society, P.O. Box 399, Longview, WA, 98632 or 360-636-5461 or email her at kbeck@teleport.com.

The **Washington State Audubon Society** office is located in Olympia at 1063 Capitol Way South. They may be contacted at 360-786-8020 or through their web site at http://www.audubon.org/chapter/wa/.

Shoalwater Birders is a group of birders who live on and bird the Long Beach Peninsula. They meet monthly and produce a monthly newsletter. For more information contact Nancy Houtzel, 360-665-6492, Susan Clark, 360-665-2753, Amy Greenhut, 360-665-3054, or Carolyn Nielson at 360-665-5974.

The **Friends of the Willapa National Wildlife Refuge** provides support and assistance to the refuge programs and enhances the awareness and appreciation of the Willapa National Wildlife Refuge. One way they accomplish this is by educating local students about the flora and fauna of the refuge. For more information, visit their web site at www.teleport.com/~mmcdowel/friendsofwillapa/ or contact President Rudy Schuver, Friends of the Willapa NWR, P.O. Box 627, Ocean Park, WA, 98640. You may call him at 360-665-6859 or email him at rudwin@willapabay.org.

The **Washington Ornithological Society** (WOS) was chartered to "increase the knowledge of the birds of Washington and enhance the communication among all persons interested in those birds." They have quarterly meetings in Seattle, publish a quarterly newsletter, *WOSNews*, have regular field trips to different parts of the state, and sponsor a Rare Bird Alert for the state, called the Bird Box. The **Bird Box** can be accessed by calling 206-281-9172. The mailing address for WOS is P. O. Box 31783, Seattle, WA, 98103-1783 or they may be contacted at http://www.wos.org

Tweeters is the Washington state birding chat line and a good place to find out more about the birds being seen in Washington. Their web address is http://www.scn.org/earth/tweeters/index.html.

North American Birds is a quarterly publication of ornithological record published by the American Birding Association. The Oregon/Washington Regional Editors of *North American Birds* are Bill Tweit (sebnabgill@aol.com) and Steve Mlodinow (sgmlod@aol.com).

A web site with information about Washington's birding hot spots is http://www.camacdonald.com/birding/uswashington.htm.

Information about pelagic trips out of Westport sponsored by Westport Seabirds is available at www.westportseabirds.com.

Information on the Breeding Bird Atlas for Washington is available at http://salmo.cqs.washington.edu/~wagap/birds/maps.html.

Christmas Bird Counts

There are four Christmas Bird Counts that cover parts of coastal Washington.

1. The Grays Harbor CBC includes Hoquiam, Ocean Shores, and Westport. The compiler is Bob Morse, who can be reached at 360-943-8600 or via email at rwmorse@home.com. The results of the last five years CBCs can be found at www.ghas.org/recentcbc.html.

2. The Leadbetter Point CBC includes much of the Long Beach Peninsula. The compiler is Robert Sudar who can be reached at 360-423-1780 or via email at fallcreek@toledotel.com.

3. The Columbia Estuary OR/WA CBC includes Fort Canby, Ilwaco, Chinook, and Fort Columbia State Park on the Washington side of the Columbia River. The compiler is Mike Patterson, who can be reached at 503-325-1365 or via email at celata@pacifier.com.

4. The Wahkiakum OR/WA CBC includes Skamokawa, Julia Butler Hansen NWR, Cathlamet, and Puget Island on the Washington side of the Columbia River. The compiler is Andrew Emlen, who can be reached at 360-795-8009 or via email at skpaddle@pacifier.com.

MORE COASTAL INFORMATION
Northwest Forest Pass

Northwest Forest Passes are now required year-round to park at specific sites in the Olympic National Forest. Passes may be acquired at participating forest service offices in Olympia, Quinault Ranger Station, and Forks Ranger Station. Annual Northwest Forest Passes cost $30.00. Day passes are $5.00.

More information on the passes is available at www.fs.fed.us/r6/olympic/onfrec/trails/trails.htm or by calling Olympic National Forest Headquarters in Olympia at 360-956-2401.

Washington Department of Fish and Wildlife Access Stewardship Decal

To keep their access sites clean, repaired, and safe, the Washingron Department of Fish and Wildlife requires an Access Stewardship Decal for parking at designated access sites throughout the state. The decal is provided free with the purchase of fishing and hunting licenses; otherwise, there is a $10.00 annual fee. Access decals can be purchased at the Department's Regional Offices, via mail, on-line, or where fishing and hunting licenses are sold. More information is available through the department's web site at www.wa.gov/wdfw/. Those sites in this guide that require an Access Stewardship Decal have been noted in the text.

Weather

Weather varies along the coast and local newspapers provide the latest forecasts. The NOAA web site at www.wrh.noaa.gov/seattle offers current weather conditions, forecasts, satellite pictures, and related information.

Tides

In summer, low tides expose tidal pools that are hidden much of the year. At these tides, the true beauty of the tide pool becomes apparent with colorful sea anemones, sea stars, barnacles, and small crabs. On the other hand, winter tides that are accompanied by strong westerly winds, can bring high tides that wash over coastal roads.

Tide tables are available in the local newspapers or can be obtained through www.harbortides.com.

Maps

A good state highway map is helpful when traveling along the coast. A free Washington State Highway Map can be obtained by contacting the Washington Department of Transportation, Communications Department, 310 Maple Park Ave SE, Olympia, WA, 98501 or by calling 360-705-7000 or through www.wsdot.wa.gov.

The **Washington Atlas and Gazetteer**, published by the DeLorme Mapping Company, is a very detailed map of every part of Washington and for those exploring new areas it is invaluable. A copy can be obtained through bookstores, outdoor supply outlets, or by contacting DeLorme Mapping Company, P. O. Box 298, Freeport, Maine, 04032, 1-800-227-1656.

Other Contacts

To learn more about tide pools, marine mammals, and information about the **Olympic Coast National Marine Sanctuary** call 360-457-NOAA (6622), or visit them at 138 W. First St. Port Angeles, WA 98362, or check their web site at www.ocnms.nos.noaa.gov.

There are two **Makah Tribal** web sites that describe tribal activities, their museum, Cape Flattery, and Neah Bay. They are www.northolympic.com/makah/index.html and www.makah.com.

Close observation of Tufted Puffin and other water birds is possible, especially during the May to early August breeding season, on boat trips out of Neah Bay to the waters around Neah Bay, Cape Flattery, and Tatoosh Island. Contact Puffin Adventures at 1-888-305-2437 or www.olypen.com/puffinadventures/.

The **Olympic Park Institute** offers a series of outdoor seminars, spring through fall, on birds, geology, forest ecology, intertidal life, marine mammals, the Pacific Northwest culture and history, arts, and backpacking among other topics. For further information, contact the Institute at 360-928-3720 or www.yni.org/opi.

Chambers of Commerce, Accommodations

Accommodations along the Washington coast may be difficult to find in summer or on holiday weekends without reservations. The most popular tourist sites are Ocean Shores, the Long Beach Peninsula, and during the fishing season, Westport, Neah Bay, Sekiu, and Ilwaco.

To assist the visiting birder in finding accommodations, in the next several pages we have provided a listing of some of the accommodations and RV parks that are available along the coast. This list has been provided by the Chambers of Commerce and Visitor Centers in Forks, Ocean Shores, Westport/Grayland, and Long Beach Peninsula. There are 7 coastal chambers of commerce along the coast and they are very helpful to visiting birders. They are:

Chamber/Visitor Center Phone	Area Covered Web Site
Clallam Bay/Sekiu 360-963-2339	Northwest Washington www.clallambay.com.
Forks 800-44-FORKS	Forks, La Push, Kalaloch www.forkswa.com.
Grays Harbor 800-321-1924	All of Grays Harbor County www.graysharbor.org.
Long Beach Peninsula Visitors Bureau 800-451-2542	Long Beach Peninsula www.funbeach.com.
Ocean Shores 800-76-BEACH	Ocean Shores www.oceanshores.org.

Raymond
360-942-5419

North Pacific County

Westport/Grayland
800-345-6223

Westport, Grayland, Tokeland
www.westportgrayland-chamber.org

The book *Northwest Coast* (see References) provides detailed coastal lodging and camping information. For anyone planning to stay along the coast, it is highly recommended.

Accomodations in the North Coast - Clallam Bay, Forks, Kalaloch, La Push, Neah Bay, Lake Ozette, Lake Quinault, and Sekiu

FORKS AREA:
FORKS • BEAVER • LA PUSH
RAIN FOREST • SOL DUC

	Rates*/Web Site*	# of Units	Credit Cards	Cabins	# Kit. Units	Guest Laundry	Pets*/with Restric.	Pool/Hot Tub	RV/# H/U
BAGBY'S TOWN MOTEL 1080 S. Forks Ave. • Forks, WA 98331 360/374-6231 • 1-800-742-2429 jani@centurytel.net *Soft, homey, & very clean rooms. Gardens with BBQ. Activities room with coffee, microwave, fitness room, tanning. Showers for campers. Some smoking units.*	$ $$ W	20	•	3	9		•	•*	
BEAR CREEK HOMESTEAD B & B 2094 Bear Creek Rd. • Port Angeles, WA 98363 • baysnger@olypen.com 360/327-3699 *Pastoral 16 acres secluded on Bear Creek. Full breakfast, private baths. furnished tents for campers. Horse packing service. 15 mi. northeast of Forks.*	$$$ W	2	•					H	
BEAR CREEK MOTEL & RV PARK P.O. Box 236 • Beaver, WA 98305 360/327-3660 • hungrybear@olypen.com *Located on Sol Duc River, satellite TV, street level. Full service restaurant adjacent, public showers, river trail. 15 miles NE of Forks.*	$ $$ $$$ W	11	•		11	1	• •*		18
BRIGHTWATER HOUSE B & B 440 Brightwater Dr. • P.O. Box 1222 Forks, WA 98331 • 360/374-5453 brightwater@olypen.com *Secluded on 60 acres with 3500' of Sol Duc River frontage. Large fireplace suite & sunny queen room with private deck. We speak fly fishing!*	$$ $$$ W	2	•						
CYCLE CAMP 1071 Mora Rd. • Forks, WA 98331 360/374-8665 • 888/552-0768 drgnass@hotmail.com *Ten seasonal camping sites for 2-wheeled travelers. Close to store, gas, cafe and beach. Single riders or groups. Support vehicles welcome.*	$ W						•*		
DEW DROP INN 100 Fernhill Rd. • P.O. Box 1996 • Forks, WA 98331 • 360/374-4055 • 1-888-433-9376 *Opened 1996. Modern, comfortable decor. 8 rooms with microwaves, refrigerators. 3 with queens, rest with extra long fulls.*	$ $$	21	•				•*		
EAGLE POINT INN B & B 384 Stormin' Norman Lane • P.O. Box 546 Beaver, WA 98305 • 360/327-3236 *Log lodge on 5 acres along the Sol Duc River. Private baths, antiques, rock fireplace. Outdoor BBQ & large lawn. Non-smoking. 10 miles north of Forks.*	$$$	3						H	
FISHERMAN'S WIDOW B & B 31 Huckleberry Lane • Forks, WA 98331 360/374-5693 fishermanswidow@centurytel.net *Private baths, non-smoking. Customized sightseeing, nature tours available. Quiet residential area.*	$$ W	2							

FORKS AREA:
FORKS • BEAVER • LA PUSH
RAIN FOREST • SOL DUC

	Rates*/Web Site*	# of Units	Credit Cards	Cabins	# Kit. Units	Guest Laundry	Pets*/with Restric.	Pool/Hot Tub	RV/# H/U
FORKS MOTEL 351 Forks Ave. S. • P.O. Box 510 • Forks, WA 98331 • 360/374-6243 • 1-800-544-3416 forksmotel@centurytel.net *73 deluxe rooms, AAA 3 diamond, jacuzzi suite, 1/2 bedroom kitchen suites. Some smoking rooms, seasonal pool, near shopping & restaurants.*	$ $$ $$$ W	73	•		8	•	•*	P	
HOH HUMM RANCH B & B 171763 Hwy. 101 • Forks, WA 98331 360/374-5337 • hohhumm@olypen.com *Large farmhouse on Hoh River 20 miles south of Forks. Many animals - a hit with children! Full farm breakfast. Shared bath. Cats in house. Non-smoking.*	$ W	3					•*		
HOH RIVER RESORT 175443 Hwy.101 • Forks, WA 98331 360/374-5566 *Level, grassy RV & camp sites under a canopy of spruce trees. Convenience store, gas, guest showers. Basic sportsmen cabins, propane heat & stove, no bedding provided.*	$	2	•	2	2	•	•		13
HUCKLEBERRY LODGE B & B 1171 Big Pine Way • Forks, WA 98331 360/374-6008 • 1-888-822-6008 hucklodge@olypen.com *Secluded on 5 pastoral acres where Roosevelt elk often visit. Fishing & adventure packages. Sauna.*	$$$ W	6	•	3	2	•		H	3
KALALOCH LODGE 157151 Hwy. 101 • Forks, WA 98331 360/962-2271 • Fax 360/962-3391 • To email: www.visitkalaloch.com *Overlooking the Pacific Ocean. Featuring cabins with or without fireplaces & kitchens. Restaurant with service bar, gift shop & mercantile store with gas.*	$$$ W	64	•	44	38		•*		
LAKE QUINAULT LODGE 345 South Shore Rd. • Quinault, WA 98575 360/288-2900 • 1-800-562-6672 • To email: www.visitlakequinault.com *Stroll the many rainforest trails near this historic 1926 lodge with dining room, lounge & gift shop. Seasonal boat rentals & massage. Groups welcome.*	$$ $$$ W	92	•				•*	P	
LAKE QUINAULT RAIN FOREST RESORT VILLAGE 516 South Shore Rd. • Quinault, WA 98575 360/288-2535 • 800/255-6936 rfr@techline.com *Fireplace cabins, motel, RV park. Salmon House Restaurant & Lounge. Home to world's largest spruce tree.*	$$ $$$ W	35	•	18	5	•			31
LAKE QUINAULT RESORT 314 North Shore Rd. • Amanda Park, WA 98526 • 360/288-2362 • 1-800-650-2362 *Peaceful, quiet getaway featuring north shore lake view frontage. Covered decks where "your" chair awaits! Seasonal boat tours.*	$$ $$$ W	9	•	1	5				

FORKS AREA:
FORKS • BEAVER • LA PUSH
RAIN FOREST • SOL DUC

	Rates*/Web Site*	# of Units	Credit Cards	Cabins	# Kit. Units	Guest Laundry	Pets/*with Restric.	Pool/Hot Tub	RV/#H/U
LA PUSH OCEAN PARK RESORT 770 Main Street • P. O. Box 67 • LaPush, WA 98350 • 360/374-5267 • 1-800-487-1267 *Ocean-front cabins, RV sites & motel. Watch whales, seabirds, launch a kayak or surfboard. Tribal ceremonies, museum, gift shop & showers.*	$ $$ $$$ W	55	•	35	55	•	•*		52
LOG CABIN RESORT 3183 East Beach Road • Port Angeles, WA 98363 • 360/928-3325 • Fax 360/928-2088 logcabin@tenforward.com *On the sunny side of Lake Crescent in Olympic National Park. Lodge rooms, chalets & cabins. Swimming, gifts, restaurant, watercraft rentals, ATM. Open 4/1-10/31.*	$$ $$$ W	28	•	8	3	•	•*		38
LONESOME CREEK RV PARK 490 Ocean Drive • P.O. Box 250 • La Push, WA 98350 • 360/374-4338 *Oceanfront RV park with convenience store, gas, ATM, showers & clubhouse. Horseshoe pits, a mile of sandy beach. Good Sam. Native American arts & crafts.*	$	•				•	•*		42
MANITOU LODGE B & B 813 Kilmer Rd. • P.O. Box 600 • Forks, WA 98331 • 360/374-6295 • Fax 360/374-7495 • manitou@olypen.com *Secluded cedar lodge on 10 forested acres. 5 minutes from Rialto Beach. All rooms with private baths. Children & pets welcome - some restrictions.*	$$ $$$ W	6	•	2			•*		
MILL CREEK INN 1061 South Forks Ave. • P.O. Box 1182 Forks, WA 98331 • grizzly@olypen.com 360/374-5873 *Small inn on Mill Creek, cable TV, private baths, smoking outside, children welcome. Full breakfast & fishing charters available.*	$ $$	2	•				•		
MILLER TREE INN B & B 654 E. Division St. • P.O. Box 1565 • Forks, WA 98331 • 360/374-6806 • 800/943-6563 • Fax 360/374-6807 MillerTreeInn@centurytel.net *Historic 1916 farmhouse in pastoral setting. Warm hospitality & breakfast abundant. Suite available for children under 7. "NW Best Places."*	$$ $$$ W	7	•		1		•*		H
MISTY VALLEY INN B & B 194894 Hwy. 101 N. • P. O. Box 2239 Forks, WA 98331 • mistyinn@olypen.com 1-877/374-9389 *Magnificent view of Sol Duc River valley in rainforest setting. 3 course gourmet breakfast on the sun deck, afternoon tea service. Children over 12 welcome.*	$$$ W	4	•						H

*Rate Range:
$ - $45 & under • **$$** - $46 to $75 • **$$$** - over $76

FORKS AREA:
FORKS • BEAVER • LA PUSH
RAIN FOREST • SOL DUC

	Rates*/Web Site*	# of Units	Credit Cards	Cabins	# Kit. Units	Guest Laundry	Pets/*with Restric.	Pool/Hot Tub	RV/#H/U
MOUNTAIN VIEW CABIN RESORT 285 Maxfield Homestead Rd. • Forks, WA 98331 • 360/374-6486 • Fax 360/374-7487 mountainviewcabins@hotmail.com *Log cabins for 2 to 8 with kitchens & baths on working ranch. Hunting, fishing, guides, driving range. 10 min. from rivers & Rialto Beach.*	$$ $$$	5	•	5	5		•*		
OLSON'S VACATION CABINS 2423 Mora Road • Forks, WA 98331 360/374-3142 *Unique, private getaway on a 4-acre meadow near Quillayute River & Rialto Beach. For up to 4-6 people, children welcome.*	$$ W	2		2	2		•	H	
OLYMPIC SUITES INN 800 Olympic Drive • Forks, WA 98331 360/374-5400 • 1-800-262-3433 olympicsuites@olypen.com *Spacious 1 & 2 bedroom suites in a quiet location near the Calawah River. Enjoy a suite at motel rates!*	$ $$ $$$ W	32	•		32	•	•*		
PACIFIC INN MOTEL 352 S. Forks Avenue • Forks, WA 98331 • 360/374-9400 • 1-800-235-7344 pacificinn@centurytel.net *Built in 1991. Frigs, microwaves, queen beds, air conditioned. Near restaurants & shopping. H/C access.*	$ $$ W	34	•			•			
RIVER INN B & B 2596 Bogachiel Way • Forks, WA 98331 • woodward@kendaco.telebyte.com 360/374-6526 *Private setting on the Bogachiel River among old growth trees & elk pastures. Covered hot tub on the riverbank. Special fishermen's rates. 2.5 mi. west of Forks.*	$$ $$$	3						H	
SHADOW MOUNTAIN CAMPGROUND 232951 Hwy. 101 • Port Angeles, WA 98363 360/928-3043 • 877/928-3043 mountain@olypen.com *Large RV sites with mountain view. Tent sites, showers, playgrnd., mini golf, gas, diesel & propane. General store & cafe. One mile east of Lake Crescent.*	$		•			•	•*		40
SHADYNOOK COTTAGE B & B 81 Ash Ave. • P.O. Box 483 • Forks, WA 98331 shadynook@forkswa.com Phone/Fax 360/374-5497 *Private, cozy cottages with "fireplaces". Victorian decor: lamps, linens & stained glass windows. Will do extra for special occasions.*	$$$ W	2		2	2				

"W" denotes lodgings with web sites at press time.
Log on at www.forkswa.com/lodging/
for current links and more information.

NORTHWEST COAST:
CLALLAM BAY • SEKIU
NEAH BAY • LAKE OZETTE

	Rates*/Website*	# of Units	Credit Cards	Cabins	# Kit. Units	Guest Laundry	Pets/*with Restric.	Pool/Hot Tub	RV/# H/U
BAY MOTEL 15562 Hwy. 112 • Sekiu, WA 98381 360/963-2444 *Phones, cable TV, restaurant adjacent. 18 miles to Makah Museum. Some water view units. Children welcome.*	$ $$	16	•		14		•*		
THE CAPE MOTEL & RV PARK 1500 Bayview Avenue • P.O. Box 136 • Neah Bay, WA 98357 • 360/645-2250 *Close to Makah Museum, marina, restaurants, and general store. Short drive to Cape Flattery and ocean beaches.*	$$	10	•	2	5	•	•*		50
CHITO BEACH RESORT 7639 Hwy. 112 • P.O. Box 270 • Clallam Bay, WA 98326 • 360/963-2581 chitobch@olypen.com *Unique location. Cozy cabins on the beach. Private bay. Full kitchens. Art gallery. Peaceful. Open all year.*	$$$ W	4		4	4				
CURLEY'S RESORT & DIVE CENTER 291 Front Street • P.O. Box 265 • Sekiu, WA 98381 • 360/963-2281 • 1-800-542-9680 curleys@olypen.com *Water view rooms, with kitchens. Non smoking rooms, phones, cable TV, river rock BBQ, gift shop, espresso, RV park, full service dive shop.*	$ $$ $$$ W	21	•	3	12		•*		10
HERB'S MOTEL & CHARTERS 411 Front St. • P.O. Box 175 • Sekiu, WA 98381 • 360/963-2346 herbs@centurytel.net *Open all year! Come relax by the sea. Cable TV, phones, view units, kitchens. Hiking, beachcombing, diving, charters.*	$ $$ $$$ W	12	•		6		•*		
HILDEN'S MOTEL 1663 Hwy. 112 • P.O. Box 181 • Neah Bay, WA 98357 • 360/645-2306 *Bullman Beach, 3 mi. east of Neah Bay. Beach front, views of Vancouver Island, Sail Rock & Seal Rock. Beachcombing, free coffee.*	$ $$ $$$	5			5				

FORKS AREA, CONT.

	Rates*/Website*	# of Units	Credit Cards	Cabins	# Kit. Units	Guest Laundry	Pets/*with Restric.	Pool/Hot Tub	RV/# H/U
SOL DUC GUEST HOUSE 654 Stormin' Norman Lane • P.O. Box 325 Beaver, WA 98305 • 360/327-3373 pbarlow@olypen.com *Secluded riverfront retreat sleeps up to 4 people. Continental breakfast with nightly rate, non-smoking, children over 8. You are our only guest!*	$$ $$$	1		1		•			
SOL DUC HOT SPRINGS RESORT Sol Duc River Rd. • P.O. Box 2169 • Port Angeles, WA 98362 • pamsdr@aol.com 360/327-3583 *In Olympic National Park. 3 hot pools & freshwater swimming pool. Massage, restaurant, deli & gifts. RV sites & cabins, seasonal, non-smoking.*	$$$ W	32	•	26	6			H P	20

Rate Range: $ - $45 & under; $$ - $46 to $75; $$$ - over $76

NORTHWEST COAST:
CLALLAM BAY • SEKIU
NEAH BAY • LAKE OZETTE

	Rates*/Website*	# of Units	Credit Cards	Cabins	# Kit. Units	Guest Laundry	Pets/*with Restric.	Pool/Hot Tub	RV/# H/U
LOST RESORT AT LAKE OZETTE 20860 Hoko-Ozette Rd. • Clallam Bay, WA 98326 • 360/963-2899 • 1-800-950-2899 lostresort@hotmail.com *"Westernmost Outpost in the Continental USA."* Borders Olympic National Park at Lake Ozette. Primitive campsites. Showers, general store, deli/tavern, microbrews, espresso.	$ W								
SHIPWRECK POINT RV PARK 6850 Hwy. 112 • Sekiu, WA 98381 360/963-2744 • shipwreck@olypen.com Beautiful sandy beach, charter booking, whale watching, fishing, scuba diving, kayak rentals. 8 miles west of Sekiu. Tent sites, seasonal.	$		•			•	•*		29
SILVER SALMON RESORT & RV PARK Bayview Ave. • P.O. Box 156 • Neah Bay, WA 98357 • 360/645-2388 • 1-888-713-6477 silvsalm@centurytel.net *Motel and RV park across from marina, close to store, cafe, laundromat and museum.*	$ $$ $$$	10	•		5		•*		12
SNOW CREEK RESORT Hwy. 112, Marker 691 • P.O. Box 248 Neah Bay, WA 98357 • 360/645-2284 **800/883-1464** *Seasonal, store, trailer rentals, showers, marina, propane, diver's air. Sightseeing tours, whale watching.*	$		•		3		•*		47
STRAITSIDE RESORT 241 Front St. • P.O. Box 135 • Sekiu, WA 98381 • 360/963-2100 • strait@olypen.com *Charming vintage cabins, suites, studios overlooking the Strait. Non-smoking, cable TV, kitchens, phones. Clean, quiet, comfy. Enchanting gardens, BBQ firepit.*	$ $$ $$$ W	7	•	2	7				
TYEE MOTEL Bayview Ave. • P.O. Box 193 • Neah Bay, WA 98357 • 360/645-2223 *Near Makah Marina, cafe & store. Great fishing, beautiful beaches. Close to renowned Makah Museum & Cape Flattery. Some water view units. Seasonal.*	$ $$ $$$	41	•		15		•		16

FORKS AREA, CONT.

	Rates*/Website*	# of Units	Credit Cards	Cabins	# Kit. Units	Guest Laundry	Pets/*with Restric.	Pool/Hot Tub	RV/# H/U
SOL DUC RIVER LODGE B & B 206114 Hy. 101 N. • P.O. Box 2617 Forks, WA 98331 • 360/327-3709 *Large, fully windowed chalet with wraparound deck on upper Sol Duc River. Full breakfast. Guide service available. 13 mi. north of Forks.*	$$ $$$	3							
THREE RIVERS RESORT 7764 La Push Rd. • Forks, WA 98331 threerivers@olypen.com • 360/374-5300 *Guide service, restaurant, showers & store. 10 campsites. Close to beaches & fishing. Call for river conditions & fishing reports.*	$ $$ W	5	•	5	4	•	•*		10

*These web sites can be visited through links at

Accommodations in Ocean Shores

Hotels & Resorts

HOTEL/MOTEL (TYPE OF UNIT OR LOCATION IF NOT IN OCEAN SHORES)	PHONE (TOLL-FREE NUMBER)	Number of Rooms	Ocean View Avail.	Indoor Pool	Outdoor Pool	Sauna or Spa	Fireplace	No-Smoking Rooms	In Room Jacuzzi's	Cable TV	Kitchen	Phone in Rooms	Pets Allowed	Handicap Access	Mgr Credit Cards	Meeting Rooms	Nightly Rates (subject to change)
Best Western Lighthouse Suites Inn	360/289-2311 1-800-757-SURF	76	♦		♦	♦	♦	♦	♦	♦	M	♦			♦	♦	♦	$100 - 199
Caroline Inn	360/289-0450	5	♦			♦	♦	♦	♦	♦	♦	♦	♦			♦		$125 - 175
Canterbury Inn CONDOMINIUM MOTEL	360/289-3317 1-800-562-6678	44	♦	♦		♦	♦	♦		♦	♦	♦		♦	♦	♦		$88 - 190
Chalet Village CABIN TYPE ACCOMMODATIONS	360/289-4297 1-800-303-4297	9	♦				♦	♦		♦	♦	♦	♦	♦		♦		$85 - 105
Chris' by the Sea	360/289-3066 1-800-446-5747	7	♦				♦		♦		♦	♦				♦		$40 - 65
Coho Motel IN WESTPORT	360/268-0111 1-800-572-0177	28	♦				♦		♦		♦		♦	♦	♦	♦	♦	$45 - 87
Days Inn	360/289-9570 1-800-DAYS INN	46	♦		♦		♦		♦	M	♦		♦	♦				$59 - 109
Discovery Inn CONDOMINIUM MOTEL	360/289-3371 1-800-882-8821	22			♦	♦	♦	♦	♦		♦	♦		♦	♦	♦	♦	$48 - 88
Echoes of the Sea IN COPALIS BEACH	360/289-3358 1-800-578-ECHO	8					♦		♦		♦	♦		♦		♦	♦	$35 - 90
Grey Gull CONDOMINIUM MOTEL	360/289-3381 1-800-562-9712	38	♦				♦	♦	♦		♦	♦	♦			♦	♦	$80 - 230
Holiday Inn Express	360/289-4900 1-888-770-7878	72	♦	♦			♦		♦	JT	♦	M	♦		♦	♦	♦	$69 - 189
Lake Quinalt Lodge OLYMPIC NATIONAL FOREST	360/288-2900	92		♦		♦	♦	♦	♦					♦	♦	♦	♦	$105 - 280
Linde's Landing	360/289-3323 1-800-448-2433	64	♦		♦	♦	♦	♦	♦		♦	♦		♦	♦	♦	♦	$75 - 209
Mr. Sandman Inn CONDOMINIUM MOTEL (OPENS MARCH 2001)	360/289-9000 1-866-289-9003	60	♦				♦	♦	♦	♦	♦	M	♦		♦	♦	♦	$89 - 249
Nautilus CONDOMINIUM MOTEL	360/289-2722 1-800-221-4541	24	♦			♦	♦	♦	♦		♦	♦			♦	♦	♦	$70 - 135
North Beach Motel IN OCEAN CITY	360/289-4116 1-800-640-8053	15					♦		♦		♦	♦		♦		♦		$45 - 85
Ocean Crest Resort IN MOCLIPS	360/276-4465 2091-800-684-VIEW	45	♦	♦		♦	♦		♦		♦			♦		♦	♦	$55 - 140
Ocean Shores Motel	360/289-3351 1-800-464-2526	40				♦	♦	♦	♦		♦	♦		♦		♦		$59 - 125
Pacific Sands IN OCEAN CITY	360/289-3588	9			♦		♦		♦		♦	♦		♦		♦		$40 - 59
Polynesian Resort	360/289-3361 1-800-562-4836	72	♦	♦		♦	♦	♦	♦		♦	♦	♦		♦	♦	♦	$79 - 199
Quality Inn	360/289-2040 1-800-228-5151	62	♦	♦		♦		♦	♦	M	♦			♦	♦	♦	♦	$65 - 169
Quinault Beach Resort	360/289-9466	159	♦	♦		♦	♦	♦	♦		♦			♦	♦	♦	♦	$89 - 700
Sand Dollar Inn & Cabins IN PACIFIC BEACH	360/276-4525	14	♦			♦	♦	♦	♦		♦	♦		♦		♦		$45 - 130
Sands Resort	360/289-2444 1-800-841-4001	152	♦	♦	♦	♦	♦	♦	♦		♦	♦			♦	♦	♦	$38 - 205
Shilo Inn	360/289-4600 1-800-222-2244	113	♦	♦		♦		♦	♦	JT	♦	M	♦		♦	♦	♦	$99 - 230
Silver King	360/289-3386 1-800-562-6001	50	♦					♦	♦		♦	♦		♦		♦		$50 - 90
Silver Waves Inn BED AND BREAKFAST	360/289-2490 1-888-257-0894	4					♦		♦						♦	♦	♦	$85 - 130
Upper Deck Suites	360/289-4555	4	♦				♦	♦	♦	♦	♦	♦				♦		$125 - 180
Vagabond House	360/289-2350 1-800-290-2899	17							♦		♦	♦		♦		♦		$39 - 220
Weatherly CONDOMINIUM MOTEL	360/289-3088 800-562-8612	15	♦			♦	♦	♦	♦		♦	♦	♦			♦	♦	$65 - 150
Westerly Motel	360/289-3711	8							♦		♦	♦		♦		♦		$30 - 69

JT = Jet Tubs   M= Mini Kitchens

Camping & RV Guide

	Full Hook-ups	Tents allowed	Restrooms	Showers	Laundry	Cable TV	Dump Station	Pets Allowed	Major Credit Cards	Rates (subject to change)
Coho RV Park 360/268-0111 or 1-800-572-0177 WESTPORT	✦		✦	✦	✦	✦	✦	✦	✦	$16
Driftwood Acre 360/289-3484 COPALIS BEACH		✦	✦	✦	✦		✦	✦	✦	$18-$30
Echoes of the Sea Motel & RV 360/289-3358 or 1-800-578-3246 COPALIS BEACH	✦	✦	✦	✦		✦	✦	✦	✦	$18
Ocean Shores Marina & RV Park 360/289-0414 or 1-800-742-0414 OCEAN SHORES	✦	✦	✦	✦	✦	✦	✦	✦	✦	$15
Ocean Shores Resort 360/289-0618 SHORES, HWY. 109 MEMBERS ONLY										
Screamin' Eagle Campground 360/289-0223 OCEAN CITY		✦	✦	✦			✦	✦	✦	$10
Surf & Sand RV Park 360/289-2707 COPALIS BEACH		✦	✦	✦	✦	✦	✦	✦	✦	$16+
Yesterday's RV Park 360/289-9227 or 360/289-3459 OCEAN SHORES		✦	✦	✦			✦	✦	✦	$10 $20

CALL OCEAN CITY STATE PARK FOR MORE INFORMATION
AT 360/289-3553 OR 1-800-233-0321.
FOR RESERVATIONS PLEASE CALL 1-800-452-5687.

Nightly Rentals

Chris' By the Sea
(360) 289-3066 or 1-800-446-5747

Beach Front Vacation Rentals
(360) 289-3568 or 1-800-544-8887

Ocean Shores Vacation Rentals
(360) 289-3211 or 1-877-319-3211

Ocean Shores Reservation Bureau
(360) 289-2430 or 1-800-562-8612

Ocean View Resort Homes
(360) 289-4416 or 1-800-927-6394

Beach Breezes
(360) 289-9690 or 1-888-422-3781

Accommodations in Westport, Grayland and Tokeland

LODGING GUIDE
Westport Grayland Tokeland
Complements of
The WESTPORT/GRAYLAND
CHAMBER OF COMMERCE
P. O. Box 306
Westport, WA 98595-0306
e-mail   westport@techline.com
1-800-345-6223 (360) 268-9422
Fax (360) 268-1990
WWW.WESTPORTGRAYLAND-CHAMBER.ORG

Revised 5/01

	Phone	Number of Rooms	Ocean or Bay View	Indoor Pool	Sauna Spa Jacuzzi Bath	Fireplaces	Non Smoking Rooms	Cable	Kitchen	Telephones in Room / TV	Pets	Handicap Allowed / Equip	Meeting Room	Credit Cards
GRAYLAND & TOKELAND MOTELS -B & B's- COTTAGES - RESORTS														
Grayland Motel & Cottages	360-267-2395 1-800-292-0845	15						■	■			■	■	■
Ocean Gate Resort	360-267-1956 1-800-473-1956	6					■	■	■			■		
Ocean Spray Motel	360-267-2205	10						■	■	■				■
Tokeland Hotel & Restaurant	360-267-7006	18	■				■						■	■
Walsh Motel & Beachfront Units	360-267-2191	24	■		■	■	■	■	■	■		■		■
WESTPORT MOTELS – RESORTS - BED & BREAKFAST														
Alaskan Motel & Apt.	268-9133 1-866-591-4154	11					■	■	■	■		■		■
Albatross Motel	360-268-9233	13					■	■	■			■		■
Breakers Motel & Go Karts	360-268-0848 1-800-898-4889	18			■	■	■	■	■			■		■
Chateau Westport	360-268-9101 1-800-255-9101	108	■	I	■	■	■	■	■			■	■	■
Chinook Motel	360-268-9623	11					■	■		■				■
Coho Motel & RV	360-268-0111 1-800-572-0177	28	■				■	■		■				■
Frank L Motel	360-268-9200	13				■	■	■	■	■		■		■
Glenacres Inn B & B	360-268-0958	8				■	■	■				■		■
Harbor Resort	360-268-0169	14	■			■	■	■				■	■	■
Holiday Motel	360-268-9356	10					■	■		■		■		■
Islander Motel & RV	268-9166 1-800-322-1740	33	■	O			■	■		■		■	■	■
Mariners Cove Inn	360-268-0531	9					■	■	■			■		■
McBee's Silver Sands	360-268-9029	19					■	■	■					■
Ocean Ave. Inn	360-268-9278 1-888-692-5262	12	■				■	■	■	■		■		■
Orca Motel	360-268-5010	8						■						■
Pacific Motel & RV	360-268-9325	12	O				■	■					■	■
Seagull's Nest	360-268-9711 1-888-613-9078	16				■	■	■	■	■				■
Shipwreck Motel	360-268-9151 1-888-225-2313	41	■				■	■		■		■		■
Surf Spray Motel	360-268-9149 1-888-600-9149	10	■			■	■	■	■	■		■		
Vacations By The Sea	1-888-FUNSAND 268-0531	120	■		■	■	■	■	■			■		■

RV GUIDE & HOUSE RENTAL
Westport Grayland Tokeland
Revised 5/01

	NUMBER OF HOOK UPS	TENT CAMPING	OCEAN OR BAY VIEW	OUTDOOR POOL	SHOWERS	CAMP FIRES	REC ROOM	PETS ALLOWED	REST ROOMS	SAUNA SPA	LAUNDRY	CABLE TV	DUMP STATION	CREDIT CARDS
GRAYLAND RV's														
Kenanna RV 360-267-3515 1-800-867-3515	90	■			■	■	■	■	■		■	■		■
Ocean Gate Resort 360-267-1956 1-800-473-1956	25	■	■		■	■	■	■	■			■		
Willapa Harbor RV 360-942-2392 In Raymond 1-877-735-9407	20				■	■	■	■	■			■	■	■
WESTPORT RV's														
American Sunset 360-268-0207 RV Resort 1-800-569-2267	120	■		O	■	■	■	■	■		■	■		■
Coho Motel & RV 360-268-0111 1-800-572-0177	76		■					■			■	■		■
Grizzly Joe's RV 360-268-5555	35		■		■			■	■		■	■		■
Holand Center 360-268-9582	80		■	■	■			■	■		■	■	■	■
Islander Motel & RV 360-268-9166 1-800-322-1740	60	■	O		■				■		■	■		■
Kila Hana Camperland 268-9528	108	50			■	■	■	■	■		■	■	■	
Pacific Motel & RV 360-268-9325	80	■		O	■	■	■	■	■		■	■	■	■
Sand & Surf RV 360-268-0817	10	■		■	■			■				■		
Surf Spray Motel & RV 268-9149 1-888-600-9149	11		■					■			■	■		■
Totem RV 360-268-0025 1-888-TOTEMRV	76	■	■		■			■	■		■	■	■	

Grayland Beach State Park & Twin Harbors State Park   1-800-452-5687 Reservations   1-800-233-0321 Information

HOUSE RENTAL - Nightly & weekly

The Beach House (509) 235-8110 Oceanfront house rental, 3 bedrooms fully furnished
Grayland, WA 1-888-822-8110 cable TV, VCR, fireplace, piano

First Cabin Ocean Front Cottage 360-267-5100 Cozy private ocean view getaway for two. Full
Grayland, WA 1-888-532-6140 Kitchen, TV, VCR , Non smoking, 300ft from the beach.

Jetty View Beach House 360-268-9602 Two story home, panoramic view of the ocean, TV, VCR
Westport, WA wayne@mail.techline.com four bedrooms, fireplace, laundry, full kitchen, sleeps 15

Simmodd Fantasy Cabins 360-267-3234 4 cabins to choose from with kitchens, BBQ and other
Grayland, WA 253-887-1165 nice amenities. Please call for more information.

Vacations By The Sea 1-888-UNSAND 268-0531 Beautiful new oceanfront 1&2 bedroom condo's with
Westport, WA. Fantastic view and close to oceanfront hiking/biking paths & lighthouse. All amenities inclu

Accommodations in Ilwaco, Klipsan Beach, Long Beach, Nahcotta, Ocean Park, Pacific Beach, and Seaview

Where to Stay: Hotels, Motels, and Cottages

	OCEAN/BAY FRONT	OCEAN/BAY VIEW	HOT TUB/SAUNA/SPA · IR = IN ROOM OS = ON SITE	POOL: IN OR OUT	KITCHENS AVAILABLE	NON-SMOKING AVAILABLE	CABLE TV	VCR AVAILABLE	FIREPLACE AVAILABLE	PETS WELCOME	CHILDREN WELCOME	PLAYGROUND	WHEELCHAIR ACCESS	MEETING ROOM	RECREATION ROOM	EXERCISE ROOM	PHONES IN ROOMS	# UNITS	RATES	PAYMENT
Anchorage Cottages 2209 Boulevard N. Long Beach, WA 98631 360-642-2351 800-646-2351 www.theanchoragecottages.com info@theanchoragecottages.com	■	■			■	■	■	■	■	■	■	■						10	58.50-112.50	CASH CHECK TRAVELERS CHK VISA MASTERCARD DISCOVER AM EXPRESS
Anthony's Home Court 1310 Pacific Hwy. N. Long Beach, WA 98631 360-642-2802 888-787-2754 www.anthonyshomecourt.com djh@anthonyshomecourt.com					■	■	■	■		■	■							8	49.95-135	CASH CHECK TRAVELERS CHK VISA MASTERCARD DISCOVER AM EXPRESS
Arcadia Court 401 N. Ocean Beach Blvd. Long Beach , WA 98631 360-642-2613 877-642-2613					■	■	■				■							8	40-99	CASH CHECK TRAVELERS CHK VISA MASTERCARD DISCOVER AM EXPRESS
Blackwood Beach Cottages 20711 Pacific Hwy. Ocean Park, WA 98640 360-665-6356 888-376-6356 www.blackwoodbeachcottages.com cottages@pacifier.com	■	■			■	■	■	■	■		■				■			10	90-159	CASH CHECK TRAVELERS CHK VISA MASTERCARD DISCOVER AM EXPRESS
Boardwalk Cottages 800 Ocean Beach Blvd. So. Long Beach, WA 98631 360-642-2305 800-569-3804 www.boardwalkcottages.com reservations@boardwalkcottages.com			OS		■	■	■	■	■		■		■					10	54-125	CASH CHECK TRAVELERS CHK VISA MASTERCARD AM EXPRESS
Boulevard Motel 301 Boulevard N. Long Beach, WA 98631 360-642-2434	■	■		IN	■		■		■	■	■	■						22	45-85	CASH CHECK TRAVELERS CHK VISA MASTERCARD DISCOVER AM EXPRESS
The Breakers Hwy. 103 at 26th Long Beach, WA 98631 360-642-4414 800-219-9833 www.breakerslongbeach.com rooms@breakerslongbeach.com	■	■	IR, OS	IN	■	■	■	■	■		■		■				■	144	39-225	CASH CHECK TRAVELERS CHK VISA MASTERCARD DISCOVER AM EXPRESS
Chautauqua Lodge 304 14th St. N. Long Beach, WA 98631 360-642-4401 800-869-8401 www.chautauqualodge.com chautldg@willapabay.org	■	■	OS	IN	■	■	■			■	■			■	■		■	180	39-179	CASH CHECK TRAVELERS CHK VISA MASTERCARD DISCOVER AM EXPRESS
Coastal Cottages 1511 264th Place Ocean Park, WA 98640 360-665-4658 800-200-0424 coastalcottages@webtv.net					■		■		■	■	■							4	55-75	CASH CHECK TRAVELERS CHK VISA MASTERCARD DISCOVER AM EXPRESS

 Long Beach Peninsula Visitors Bureau 1-800-451-2542 • www.funbeach.com

Where to Stay: Hotels, Motels, and Cottages

	Ocean/Bay Front	Ocean/Bay View	Hot Tub/Sauna/Spa (IR=In Room, OS=On Site)	Pool: In or Out	Kitchens Avail.	Non-Smoking Avail.	Cable TV	VCR Avail.	Fireplace Avail.	Pets Welcome	Children Welcome	Playground	Wheelchair Access	Meeting Room	Recreation Room	Exercise Room	Phones in Rooms	# Units	Rates	Payment
Eagle's Nest Resort 700 W. Northhead Rd. Ilwaco, WA 98624 360-642-8351 www.eaglesnestresort.com eaglenr@pacifier.com		■	OS	IN	■	■	■	■			■		■	■		■		25	50-200	CASH, CHECK, TRAVLERS CHK, VISA, MASTERCARD, DISCOVER, AM EXPRESS
Edgewater Inn 409 S.W. 10th St. Long Beach, WA 98631 360-642-2311 800-561-2456	■	■					■	■			■		■	■			■	84	49-139	CASH, CHECK, TRAVLERS CHK, VISA, MASTERCARD, DISCOVER, AM EXPRESS
Harbor Lights Motel 147 Howerton (Port of Ilwaco) Ilwaco, WA 98624 360-642-3196	■	■					■	■		■								19	30-68.50	CASH, CHECK, TRAVLERS CHK, VISA, MASTERCARD, DISCOVER, AM EXPRESS
Heidi's Inn 126 Spruce St. Ilwaco, WA 98624 360-642-2387 800-576-1032 heidiinn@willapabay.org			OS		■	■	■	■			■						■	25	35-115	CASH, CHECK, TRAVLERS CHK, VISA, MASTERCARD, DISCOVER, AM EXPRESS
Klipsan Beach Cottages 22617 Pacific Hwy. Ocean Park, WA 98640 360-665-4888 www.klipsanbeachcottages.com	■	■			■	■	■	■	■		■							8	80-115	CASH, CHECK, TRAVLERS CHK, VISA, MASTERCARD, DISCOVER, AM EXPRESS
Lighthouse Motel 12415 Pacific Way Long Beach, WA 98631 360-642-3622 877-220-7555 www.lighthousemotel.net	■	■			■	■	■	■	■		■						■	21	54.50-159	CASH, CHECK, TRAVLERS CHK, VISA, MASTERCARD, DISCOVER, AM EXPRESS
Ocean Lodge 1 & 2 208 Bolstad Ave. W. Long Beach, WA 98631 360-642-5400	■	■	OS	OUT	■	■	■	■	■		■		■		■		■	65	45-105	CASH, CHECK, TRAVLERS CHK, VISA, MASTERCARD, DISCOVER, AM EXPRESS
Ocean Park Resort 25904 R St. Ocean Park, WA 98640 360-665-4585 800-835-4634 www.opresort.com info@opresort.com			OS	OUT	■						■	■	■	■	■	■		14	55-110	CASH, CHECK, TRAVLERS CHK, VISA, MASTERCARD, DISCOVER, AM EXPRESS
Our Place at the Beach 1309 S. Ocean Beach Blvd. Long Beach, WA 98631 360-642-3793 800-538-5107 www.ohwy.com/wa/o/ourplace.htm tompson@aone.com		■	OS		■	■	■	■	■		■			■	■	■	■	25	39-84	CASH, CHECK, TRAVLERS CHK, VISA, MASTERCARD, DISCOVER, AM EXPRESS

Where to Stay:
Hotels, Motels, and Cottages ⚓

	OCEAN/BAY FRONT	OCEAN/BAY VIEW	HOT TUB/SAUNA/SPA (IR = IN ROOM, OS = ON SITE)	POOL	KITCHENS AVAILABLE	NON-SMOKING AVAILABLE	CABLE TV	VCR AVAILABLE	FIREPLACE AVAILABLE	PETS WELCOME	CHILDREN WELCOME	PLAYGROUND	WHEELCHAIR ACCESS	MEETING ROOM	RECREATION ROOM	EXERCISE ROOM	PHONES IN ROOMS	# UNITS	RATES	PAYMENT
Pacific View Motel 205 Bolstad Ave. W. Long Beach, WA 98631 360-642-2415 800-238-0859 www.willapabay.org/~pacvu pacvu@willapabay.org	●		IR		●	●	●			●	●		●				●	19	45-150	● CASH ● CHECK ● TRAVLERS CHK ● VISA ● MASTERCARD ● DISCOVER ● AM EXPRESS
Sand-Lo Motel 1910 Pacific Hwy. N. Long Beach , WA 98631 360-642-2600 800-676-2601					●	●			●	●							●	10	42-75	● CASH ● CHECK ● TRAVLERS CHK ● VISA ● MASTERCARD ● DISCOVER ● AM EXPRESS
Seaview Coho Motel 3701 Pacific Way Seaview , WA 98644 360-642-2531 800-681-8153 cohoseaview@juno.com					●	●	●		●		●		●					13	35-110	● CASH ● CHECK ● TRAVLERS CHK ● VISA ● MASTERCARD ● DISCOVER ● AM EXPRESS
Seaview Motel and Cottages Seaview Beach Approach and Pacific Hwy. Seaview, WA 98644 360-642-2450 www.beachdog.com jim@beachdog.com					●	●	●			●	●							14	36-85	● CASH ● CHECK ● TRAVLERS CHK ● VISA ● MASTERCARD ● DISCOVER ● AM EXPRESS
Shakti Cove Cottages 25301 Park Ave. Ocean Park, WA 98640 360-665-4000 www.shakticove.com shakti@aone.com					●	●	●	●	●	●	●							11	65-110	● CASH ● CHECK ● TRAVLERS CHK ● VISA ● MASTERCARD ● DISCOVER ● AM EXPRESS
Shaman Motel 115 3rd St. S.W. Long Beach, WA 98631 360-642-3714 800-753-3750 www.wilbay.com citizenkdm@netscape.net			OUT	●	●	●		●	●	●							●	42	54-94	● CASH ● CHECK ● TRAVLERS CHK ● VISA ● MASTERCARD ● DISCOVER ● AM EXPRESS
Historic Sou'wester Lodge, Cabins, & TCH TCH! Beach Access Rd. (38th PL.) Seaview, WA 98644 360-642-2542 www.souwesterlodge.com souwester@willapabay.org	●	●			●	●	●	●	●	●	●		●					24	39-129	● CASH ● CHECK ● TRAVLERS CHK ● VISA ● MASTERCARD ● DISCOVER ● AM EXPRESS
Sunset View Resort 25517 Park Ave. Ocean Park, WA 98640 360-665-4494 www.washingtoncoast.com 800-272-9199 sunsetview@willapabay.org	●	●	OS		●	●	●		●		●	●	●				●	52	51-187	● CASH ● CHECK ● TRAVLERS CHK ● VISA ● MASTERCARD ● DISCOVER ● AM EXPRESS
Super 8 Motel 500 Ocean Beach Blvd. Long Beach, WA 98631 360-642-8988 888-478-3297						●	●	●			●		●				●	50	54-89	● CASH ● CHECK ● TRAVLERS CHK ● VISA ● MASTERCARD ● DISCOVER ● AM EXPRESS
The Whales Tale Motel and Book Shop 620 S. Pacific Hwy. Long Beach, WA 98631 360-642-3455 800-55-WHALE www.thewhalestale.com			OS		●	●	●		●	●	●		●				●	8	29-70	● CASH ● CHECK ● TRAVLERS CHK ● VISA ● MASTERCARD ● DISCOVER ● AM EXPRESS

🐚 Where to Stay: Bed and Breakfasts ⚓

	OCEAN/BAY FRONT	OCEAN/BAY VIEW	HOT TUB/SAUNA AVAILABLE IR = IN ROOM OS = ON SITE	CABLE TV AVAILABLE	VCR AVAILABLE	FIREPLACE AVAILABLE	NON-SMOKING	PETS WELCOME	CHILDREN WELCOME	WHEELCHAIR ACCESS	MEETING ROOM	RESTAURANT	BREAKFAST FULL OR CONTINENTAL	# ROOMS W/SHARED BATH	# ROOMS W/PRIVATE BATH	RATES	PAYMENT
Boreas Bed and Breakfast Inn 607 N. Ocean Beach Blvd. Long Beach, WA 98631 360-642-8069 888-642-8069 www.boreasinn.com boreas@boreasinn.com	■	■	IR, OS		■	■	■				■		FULL	0	5	125-135	CASH, CHECK, TRAVELERS CHK, VISA, MASTERCARD, DISCOVER, AM EXPRESS
Caswell's On The Bay 25204 Sandridge Rd. Ocean Park, WA 98640 360-665-6535 www.caswellsinn.com bcaswell@willapabay.org	■	■				■	■						FULL	0	5	110-160	CASH, CHECK, TRAVELERS CHK, VISA, MASTERCARD, AM EXPRESS
Charles Nelson Guest House 26205 Sandridge Rd. Ocean Park, WA 98640 360-665-3016 888-862-9756 www.charlesnelsonbandb.com cnbandb@charlesnelsonbandb.com		■				■	■		■		■		FULL	0	3	115-135	CASH, CHECK, TRAVELERS CHK, VISA, MASTERCARD, AM EXPRESS
China Beach Retreat P.O. Box 537 Ilwaco, WA 98624 360-642-5660 800-466-1896 www.chinabeachretreat.com innkeeper@chinabeachretreat.com	■	■	IR			■	■				■		FULL	0	3	189-239	CASH, CHECK, TRAVELERS CHK, VISA, MASTERCARD, DISCOVER, AM EXPRESS
Coast Watch Bed & Breakfast P.O. Box 841 Ocean Park, WA 98640-0841 360-665-6774 www.willapabay.org/~kmj/cw kmj@willapabay.org	■	■				■	■						CONT	0	2	99	CASH, CHECK, TRAVELERS CHK, VISA, MASTERCARD, DISCOVER, AM EXPRESS
The DoveShire 21914 Pacific Hwy. Ocean Park, WA 98640 360-665-3017 888-553-2320 www.doveshire.com doveshire@willapabay.org			OS	■	■		■						FULL	0	4	100-120	CASH, CHECK, TRAVELERS CHK, VISA, MASTERCARD, DISCOVER, AM EXPRESS
The Haskel House 12011 Pacific Way Long Beach, WA 98631 360-642-4306 www.haskelhouse.com hhouse@pacifier.com	■	■				■	■	■	■				CONT	0	3	100-110	CASH, CHECK, TRAVELERS CHK, VISA, MASTERCARD, DISCOVER, AM EXPRESS
The Inn at Ilwaco 120 Williams Ave. N.E. Ilwaco, WA 98624 360-642-8686 888-244-2523 www.longbeachlodging.com bussone@aone.com						■	■		■		■		FULL	0	9	79-189	CASH, CHECK, TRAVELERS CHK, VISA, MASTERCARD, DISCOVER, AM EXPRESS

🐚 Where to Stay: Bed and Breakfasts ⚓

	OCEAN/BAY FRONT	OCEAN/BAY VIEW	HOT TUB/SAUNA AVAILABLE IR = IN ROOM OS = ON SITE	CABLE TV AVAILABLE	VCR AVAILABLE	FIREPLACE AVAILABLE	NON-SMOKING	PETS WELCOME	CHILDREN WELCOME	WHEELCHAIR ACCESS	MEETING ROOM	RESTAURANT	BREAKFAST FULL OR CONTINENTAL	# ROOMS W/SHARED BATH	# ROOMS W/PRIVATE BATH	S RATES	PAYMENT
Lion's Paw Inn 3310 Pacific Hwy. So. Seaview , WA 98644 360-642-2481 800-972-1046 www.thelionspawinn.com lionspaw@pacifier.com			OS				■	■					FULL	2	2	60-110	● CASH ● CHECK ● TRAVELERS CHK ● VISA ● MASTERCARD ● DISCOVER ● AM EXPRESS
Moby Dick Hotel & Oyster Farm 25814 Sandridge Rd. Nahcotta, WA 98637 360-665-4543 www.nwplace.com/mobydick.html mobydickhotel@willapabay.org	■	■	OS	■	■	■	■	■	■			■	FULL	8	1	75-115	● CASH ● CHECK ● TRAVELERS CHK ● VISA ● MASTERCARD ● AM EXPRESS
The Rebecca Inn & Catering 161 Howerton Ave. Ilwaco, WA 98624 360-642-4899 888-692-6268 www.rebeccainn.com rinn@pacifier.com	■		IR	■	■	■	■				■		CONT	0	2	79-129	● CASH ● CHECK ● TRAVELERS CHK ● VISA ● MASTERCARD ● DISCOVER ● AM EXPRESS
Scandinavian Gardens Inn B & B 1610 California Ave. SW Long Beach, WA 98631 360-642-8877 800-988-9277 www.longbeachwa.com sginn@longbeachwa.com			OS				■						FULL	0	5	78.75-165	● CASH ● CHECK ● TRAVELERS CHK ● VISA ● MASTERCARD ● DISCOVER ● AM EXPRESS
The Shelburne Inn 4415 Pacific Hwy. Seaview, WA 98644 360-642-2442 800-INN-1896 www.theshelburneinn.com innkeeper@theshelburneinn.com						■	■		■	■	■	■	FULL	0	15	109-189	● CASH ● CHECK ● TRAVELERS CHK ● VISA ● MASTERCARD ● AM EXPRESS
Whalebone House 2101 Bay Ave. Ocean Park, WA 98640 360-665-5371 888-298-3330 www.whalebonehouse.com whalebone@willapabay.org						■	■						FULL	0	4	95-105	● CASH ● CHECK ● TRAVELERS CHK ● VISA ● MASTERCARD ● DISCOVER ● AM EXPRESS

Bed, Beach & Breakfast Inns: www.bedbeachbreakfast.com
"A Slow Waltz in Beach-time..."

 Long Beach Peninsula Visitors Bureau 1-800-451-2542 • www.funbeach.com ⭐

Where to Stay:
RV Parks and Tent Camping

	OCEAN/BAY FRONT	OCEAN/BAY VIEW	POOL: IN OR OUT	CABLE TV	PETS WELCOME	CHILDREN WELCOME	PLAYGROUND	MEETING ROOM	RECREATION ROOM	PUBLIC PHONES	WASHER/DRYER	SHOWERS	GROCERIES	PROPANE	# SITES	# FULL HOOKUPS	#TENT SITES	RATES	PAYMENT
Aloha RV Court Sandridge Rd. and 30th St. Seaview, WA 98644 360-642-8109 www.aloharvcourt.20m.com aloharvcourt@mail.com					●	●	●				●	●			18	18	6	18-20	CASH CHECK TRAVELERS CHK VISA MASTERCARD DISCOVER AM EXPRESS
Andersen's on the Ocean 1400 138th St. Long Beach, WA 98631 360-642-2231 800-645-6795 www.andersensrv.com info@andersensrv.com	●	●		●	●	●	●	●	●	●	●	●	●		60	60	0	22-27	CASH CHECK TRAVELERS CHK VISA MASTERCARD DISCOVER AM EXPRESS
Anthony's Home Court 1310 Pacific Hwy. N. Long Beach, WA 98631 360-642-2802 888-787-2754 www.anthonyshomecourt.com djh@anthonyshomecourt.com				●	●	●			●	●	●	●			25	25	0	15-25	CASH CHECK TRAVELERS CHK VISA MASTERCARD DISCOVER AM EXPRESS
Beacon Charters & RV Park East end Ilwaco Harbour Village Ilwaco, WA 98624 360-642-2138 877-642-6414 www.beaconcharters.com beacon.charters@usa.net	●	●								●	●	●			60	50	12	10-20	CASH CHECK TRAVELERS CHK VISA MASTERCARD DISCOVER AM EXPRESS
Driftwood RV Park 1512 N. Pacific Long Beach, WA 98631 360-642-2711 888-567-1902 www.driftwood-rvpark.com email@driftwood-rvpark.com				●	●	●	●			●	●	●			55	55	0	20.50	CASH CHECK TRAVELERS CHK VISA MASTERCARD DISCOVER AM EXPRESS
Eagle's Nest Resort 700 W. Northhead Rd. Ilwaco, WA 98624 360-642-8351 www.eaglesnestresort.com eaglenr@pacifier.com			IN	●	●	●	●	●	●	●	●	●	●	●	80	80	0	25-40	CASH CHECK TRAVELERS CHK VISA MASTERCARD DISCOVER AM EXPRESS
Evergreen Court 22212 North Pacific Ocean Park, WA 98640 360-665-6351					●	●	●				●	●			34	34	10	14-16	CASH CHECK TRAVELERS CHK VISA MASTERCARD DISCOVER AM EXPRESS
Fisherman's Cove RV Park 411 2nd Ave. SW Ilwaco, WA 98624 360-642-3689 877-COVE-RV9					●	●				●		●			53	53	10	10-20	CASH CHECK TRAVELERS CHK VISA MASTERCARD DISCOVER AM EXPRESS
Ma & Pa's Pacific RV Park 10515 Pacific Hwy. Long Beach, WA 98631 360-642-3253 www.willapabay.org/~mazie_rv mazie_rv@willapabay.org	●	●		●	●	●	●	●	●	●	●	●	●	●	50	40	20	20	CASH CHECK TRAVELERS CHK VISA MASTERCARD DISCOVER AM EXPRESS

Where to Stay:
RV Parks and Tent Camping

	OCEAN/BAY FRONT	OCEAN/BAY VIEW	POOL: IN OR OUT	CABLE TV	PETS WELCOME	CHILDREN WELCOME	PLAYGROUND	MEETING ROOM	RECREATION ROOM	PUBLIC PHONES	WASHER/DRYER	SHOWERS	GROCERIES	PROPANE	# SITES	# FULL HOOKUPS	# TENT SITES	RATES	PAYMENT
Oban Vista RV Park 1707 E. Highway 101 S. Ilwaco, WA 98624 360-642-8600 888-895-8664 obanrv@pacifier.com		✓		✓	✓	✓	✓	✓			✓	✓	✓		90	20	54	16-22	• CASH • CHECK • TRAVELERS CHK • VISA • MASTERCARD • DISCOVER • AM EXPRESS
Ocean Bay Mobile and RV Park 2515 Bay Ave. Ocean Park, WA 98640 360-665-6933				✓	✓	✓						✓			19	11	8	12-18	• CASH • CHECK • TRAVELERS CHK • VISA • MASTERCARD • DISCOVER • AM EXPRESS
Ocean Park Resort 25904 R St. Ocean Park , WA 98640 360-665-4585 800-835-4634 www.opresort.com info@opresort.com		OUT	✓	✓	✓	✓	✓	✓	✓	✓	✓	✓	✓		80	80	7	19-21	• CASH • CHECK • TRAVELERS CHK • VISA • MASTERCARD • DISCOVER • AM EXPRESS
Oceanic RV Park South 5th St. & Pacific Hwy. Long Beach, WA 98631 360-642-3836 oceanic@aone.com				✓	✓	✓				✓		✓	✓		20	20	0	13-18	• CASH • CHECK • TRAVELERS CHK • VISA • MASTERCARD • DISCOVER • AM EXPRESS
Pioneer RV Park 102 Pioneer Rd. E. Long Beach, WA 98631 360-642-3990 888-467-2615 www.willapabay.org/~pioneerrv pioneerrv@willapabay.org				✓	✓	✓					✓	✓	✓		37	33	4	19.50	• CASH • CHECK • TRAVELERS CHK • VISA • MASTERCARD • DISCOVER • AM EXPRESS
Sand-Lo Trailer Park 1910 Pacific Hwy. N. Long Beach , WA 98631 360-642-2600 800-676-2601				✓	✓	✓					✓	✓	✓		15	15	5	18	• CASH • CHECK • TRAVELERS CHK • VISA • MASTERCARD • DISCOVER • AM EXPRESS
Sandcastle RV Park 1100 N. Pacific Hwy. Long Beach, WA 98631 360-642-2174					✓	✓					✓	✓	✓		38	38	5	20-25	• CASH • CHECK • TRAVELERS CHK • VISA • MASTERCARD • DISCOVER • AM EXPRESS
Historic Sou'wester Lodge, Cabins, RV Park Beach Access Rd. (38th PL.) Seaview, WA 98644 360-642-2542 www.souwesterlodge.com souwester@willapabay.org	✓			✓	✓	✓		✓	✓		✓	✓			50	50	8	17.95-26.95	• CASH • CHECK • TRAVELERS CHK • VISA • MASTERCARD • DISCOVER • AM EXPRESS
Thousand Trails / NACO 2215 Willows Rd. Seaview, WA 98644 360-642-3091 800-642-0579 willows@willapabay.org				✓	✓	✓	✓	✓	✓	✓	✓	✓	✓	✓	120	120	60	16-20	• CASH • CHECK • TRAVELERS CHK • VISA • MASTERCARD • DISCOVER • AM EXPRESS

Where to Stay:
 ## Vacation Rental Homes

Affordable Getaway
13802 N. St. • Long Beach, WA 98631
360-896-6796 • 800-672-8105 • McBgetaway@aol.com

It's a duplex and each side has 2 bdrm, 1 bath, queen hide-a-bed, cable TV/ VCR. Located in the heart of the peninsula, mid-way between Long Beach & Ocean Park, on the ocean side with a short walk to the beach. Sleeps up to 6. Summer rates per night: $85-4, $100-5, $115-6 persons. Fully equipped: dishwasher, microwave, washer/dryer, large deck and yard with propane BBQ.

Alderedge
1403 255th Lane • Ocean Park, WA 98640
360-665-2600 • 800-665-4775 • cindyq@transport.com

Newly remodeled 1932 Ocean Park cottage, close to town. One block from Ocean Park Festival grounds. Sleeps eight, one bathroom with shower. All linens, towels, kitchen utensils supplied. Fireplace and outdoor fire pit. No pets or smoking. $90.00/night, $500.00/week up to 4 people. $10.00 each add'l person per night. $100.00 min. deposit upon reservation and $25.00 min. cleaning charge.

Beach It! Vacation Rental Service
11409 Pacific Way• Long Beach, WA 98631 • 360-642-4697
www.vacationspot.com • jklein@pacifier.com

We offer a variety of private vacation homes, from century old traditionals to a 3 story ocean front contemporary. All homes are on the west side of the highway and are either ocean front or easy beach access. Amenities include: fireplaces, jacuzzi, washers, dryers, phones, TV, VCR, decks and fully equipped kitchens. The homes sleep 2-14. So come to the Peninsula, enjoy the perfect beach home and Beach It!

Bev's Beach Bungalow
1101 34th St. • Seaview, WA 98644 • 360-642-3544
www.pacifier.com/~bevrolfe • bevrolfe@pacifier.com

Very clean, fully equipped, 20'X22' bungalow, fenced yard, in quiet Seaview. Queen bed and full size sleeper sofa; sleeps 4+. Pets and children welcome; smokers welcome but please smoke outside. $50/night for 2; $5 each add'l person. Comments from the guestbook: The best! A peaceful escape. Loved this little retreat. A wonderful, gracious hostess. My 6th visit-it's like coming home!

Coast Properties Vacation Rental Managers
400 A SW 17th St. • Long Beach, WA 98631
360-642-3414 • 360-460-7153
www.pacifier.com/~coastprp • coastprp@pacifier.com

Selection of well-maintained, fully equipped oceanfront & residential vacation homes. Amenities include TV/VCR, microwaves, W/D, fireplaces and BBQs. Some RV hookups avail. for add'l charge. All non-smoking/no pets unless prior approval. Two-night min.stay (add'l ngts may be required during special events/major holidays.) Weekly rates avail. and summer/winter rates. Rustic beach cabin to modern condo - we have it! YOUR SATISFACTION IS OUR GOAL!

Espey Place
1315 45th Pl. • Seaview, WA 98644 • 360-665-6376
800-541-2806 • www.homestead.com/espeyplace/espey1.html
bombay@willapabay.org

Minutes from Long Beach, Espey Place is a 3 bedroom, 2 bath cottage that sleeps 2 to 7. Everything is furnished: all linens, kitchenware, washer/ dryer, BBQ, VCR. Enjoy a country kitchen, large covered porch, big yard & proximity to shopping, restaurants & the beach. Charming, clean, nicely furnished. Non smoking, no pets. RATES (for 2-4): May to Sept: $100/ night; Oct to April: $65/night. Weekly discounts.

Hewitt House
3812 "J" Place • Seaview, WA 98644 • 503-284-7382 • 360-642-3685

3 bdrm historic (1887) home on the ocean front. Completely furnished, sleeps 8-10. Fireplace, TV, microwave, phone, tub/shower,washer/dryer. $70.00-$80.00 per day, weekly rates.

Jo's Vacation Rentals
1005 49th St. • Seaview, WA 98644
360-642-4958 • 800-713-2520-02

Properties sleep 1-10; on or very near ocean; all non-smoking, no pets. Some ocean view, fireplaces, stables for horses. $65 - $250.

Ocean Breeze
Ocean Park Area • Ocean Park, WA 98640
360-642-4549 • 888-879-5479
www.pacreal.com/vacation • prpm@pacreal.com

Ocean view! Short walk to the beach! 3 bedrooms, 2 bath home (2 king, 1 dbl, 1 twin). Kitchen w/microwave. Includes fireplace, TV, VCR, Gas BBQ, washer/dryer, linens. Deck, 2 car garage. NO SMOKING,NO PETS. Sleeps 1-6 Min. stay required. Priced by group size (+cleaning, tax & sec. deposit) Apr 15-Sept 15 $125-$165/night or $625-$825/week; Sept 16-Apr14 $100-$140/night or $500-$700/week.

Oceanfront Getaways
P.O. Box 214 • Ocean Park, WA 98640 • 360-665-3633
www.willapabay.org/~beachcom • beachcom@willapabay.org

2-5 bedroom oceanfront homes, fully equipped kitchens, towels and linens provided. Fireplaces, phones, TV/VCR/CD/Tape players, grills, outdoor decks & porches, great views, impeccably clean. Sleep 2-17, $95-385. No smoking, some pets OK. Located between Long Beach and Ocean Park.

Pacific Realty Property Management
102 N. Bolstad • Long Beach, WA 98631
360-642-4549 • 888-879-5479
www.pacreal.com/vacation • prpm@pacreal.com

Featuring a wide selection of rental properties from beach to bay including Ocean Breeze, Pheasant Bay House, Sandcastle and Windward Passage (see individual listings). We also manage long term home/condo rentals and screen tenants.

Paulson's Playhouse
27301 "I" Street • Ocean Park, WA 98640
503-861-2288 • 800-535-8767 • epaulson@lektro.com

Ocean front mobile home on 100'x100' lot, deadend street. Walk a few paces from the front porch and you're on the beach. Excellent for kids and relaxation. Fairly private area, 2 bedrooms, 1 bath, TV/VCR, W & D, fully furnished.

Pheasant Bay House
Willapa Bay side, Nahcotta area • 360-642-4549 • 888-879-5479
www.pacreal.com/vacation • prpm@pacreal.com

Beautiful home on 3 acres facing Willapa Bay - 4 bed, 2 baths (4 queen, 1 hide-a bed). Sleeps 1-10. Modern kitchen, gas fireplace & BBQ, cable TV, VCR, pool table, washer/dryer, linens. Dbl carport. Catch & release trout pond. NO PETS. Min. stay required (varies). Priced by group size (+cleaning, tax & sec. deposit) Apr 15-Sept 15 $150-$230/night or $750-$1150/week Sept 16-Apr14 $135-$215/night or $625-$1075/week.

Rose Cottage
48th and L Place • Seaview, WA 98644
360-642-3254 • patti@pacifier.com

Charming studio cottage in historic Seaview, surrounded by gardens featured in Sunset Magazine. Continental breakfast included. Can pick fruit/ vegetables in the garden, fresh eggs daily. Bicycles/BBQ provided. TV/ VCR available. $75-$85. Pets welcome. No credit cards accepted.

Sandcastle
Klipsan Beach • Ocean Park, WA 98640 • 360-642-4549 • 888-879-5479
www.pacreal.com/vacation • prpm@pacreal.com

Short walk to beach! Family reunion? Sleeps up to 14! 3 bed, 1 bath home (1 dbl bed, 3 dbl/town bunks) + 1 bed, 1 bath cottage (dbl/twin bunk). Kitchen w/microwave. Cable TV, BBQ, washer/dryer, linens. NO SMOKING, NO PETS. 2 RV hookups avail. (each $25/ngt.) Min. stay required.

 Long Beach Peninsula Visitors Bureau 1-800-451-2542 • www.funbeach.com

Where to Stay:
Vacation Rental Homes

Price by group size (+ cleaning, tax & sec. deposit): Apr 15-Sept 15 $200-$240/ngt or $1000-$1200/wk; Sept 16-Apr 14 $185-$245/ngt or $925-$1200/wk

Secret Garden Guesthouse
1214 246th St. • Ocean Park, WA 98640 • 503-231-5608
Secluded ranch-style house among giant rhododendrons and pines, 1/2 block from beach just south of Ocean Park. Fully furnished, paneled in knotty pine, decorated with vintage ambiance. Sleeps 8: 3 bedrooms plus hide-a-bed in living room.1 bathroom, tub/shower; fully equipped kitchen w/microwave, dishwasher, crab pot; cable TV/VCR, fireplace w/ wood; deck; BBQ. $100 night, 2 night min. 25% discount for full week.

Solstice
45th Place and "L" • Seaview, WA 98644 • 425-335-1368
www.jetcity.com/~rkr • rkr@jetcity.com
A wonderful retreat in any season, this charming 3 bedroom home sleeps 6-8. Located in historic Seaview, it's a short walk to the beach & wonderful restaurants. You & your pet will enjoy the privacy, cozy atmosphere, gas fireplace, decks, large fenced yard, herb & flower gardens & many amenities.

The Kite House
168th Place • Long Beach, WA 98631 • 206-524-5655
www.das1.iooctive.com/~msteele/kitehouse/index.html • msteele@cmc.net
1,600 sq.ft., architecturally designed oceanfront home, 5 miles north of Long Beach, secluded, perfect for family fun, romantic getaway and retreats; 3 bedrooms, 2 baths, expansive living, dining, recreation and deck areas, all with ocean views;fully equipped, state of the art quality. Sleeps 1-8. $1400.00 per week/ in season; 3 day min. off season. No smoking/ No pets. Deposit required. Call for bookings and brochure.

The Thorsen House
1005 49th St. • Seaview, WA 98644
360-642-4958 • 800-713-2520-02
4 bedroom, 3 bath, sleeps 1-10. 5 min. walk thru dunes to ocean. No pets/smoking. Elegant 1902 interior, leaded glass & sculptured walnut throughout home. 2 fireplaces, claw-foot tub off master, French parlor wood stove in kitchen. $150 refundable cleaning/security deposit.

The Western Downs
11501 Pacific Hwy. • Long Beach, WA 98631 • 360-665-3633
http://vacationparadise.com/vr/WA/sh-westerndowns.html
beachcom@willapabay.org
2 BR oceanfront home, fully furnished kitchen, towels and linens, bath with shower, new appliances, carpets and furnishings, phone, VCR CD/Radio/ Tape player, grill, deck, games, videos, garage, panoramic view, private beach path thru 4 acres of natural dunes. Sleeps 4, $95-$155. No smoking, no pets, no children under 10. Located 1 mile north of Long Beach.

The Yett Beach House
601 N. Ocean Beach Blvd. • Long Beach, WA 98631
360-642-8069 • 888-642-8069
www.boreasinn.com/yetthouse.html • boreas@boreasinn.com
5 blks. N. of the main beach approach. About 115 yrs. old, this 3 BR/1 BA picturesque cottage sits in dunes, 5 min. walk to beach. FE kitchen, sleeps 6, fireplace, linens, non-smoking, kids/pets welcome, 2 day min. Picket fenced yard, bear claw tub, covered porches. $115/day, $750/ week, major cards accepted.

Tryons by the Beach
2209 60th St. • Long Beach, WA 98631
360-642-4090 • pinky@willapabay.org
Just bring your toothbrush! Everything provided! Fully furnished. 2 bedrooms/2 baths-sleeps 7. Gas fireplace in living room. Barbeque on front deck. TV/VCR, washer/dryer, garage. Conveniently located one mile east of downtown Long Beach. $100-$135. Pets welcome with a $10 deposit/pet.

Wellington's Cove
400 Blvd S. • Long Beach, WA 98631
360-642-4979 • www.pacifier.com/~coastprp
Our 2 bedroom home is nestled in the heart of downtown Long Beach. Our house is fully furnished; each bedroom with king sized beds, queen size sleeper sofa in the living room,TV, VCR. Kitchen has jennaire stove, dishwasher and microwave. One bathroom with tub shower combination and washer & dryer. Sleeps 6 comfortably. Winter rates $115.00. Summer $139.00.

Windward Passage
501 Shoreview Drive So. • Long Beach, WA 98631 • 360-642-4549
888-879-5479 • www.pacreal.com/vacation • prpm@pacreal.com
The beach at your doorstep! Front row seats for SandSations, Kite Festival or clamming! Great for storm watchers too! Beautiful, newer 1-2 bedroom, 1-2 bath oceanfront condos. Modern FE kitchens w/microwave; some fireplaces; TV, VCR washer/dryer, linens etc. Carport. NO SMOKING, NO PETS. Priced by group size & number of bedrooms. Minimum stay required (varies).

Winkler Condo at the Surfside Inn
31512 J Place • Ocean Park, WA 98640 • 800-444-7475
800-607-3838 • www.pruteam.com • winkler@pruteam.com
Panoramic ocean view from this quality condo sitting high on the bluffs overlooking the ocean. Indoor pool, spa, golf, children's play area, trout fishing, deep sea fishing nearby. One bedroom condo features 2 full baths, queen bed & queen hideabed. Full size kitchen w/microwave. Fireplace, entertainment center, gas grill on deck. $69 to $120/night.

Camping

The are numerous campgrounds along the Washington coast managed by the Olympic National Park, Washington State Parks, Olympic National Forest, Washington Department of Natural Resources, as well as private campgrounds. A number of these facilities are closed in winter and the most popular ones can be crowded in summer, over holiday weekends, or during spring break. Reservations are encouraged.

The **Olympic National Park campgrounds** along the coast are:

Ozette, at Lake Ozette
Graves Creek, E. of Lake Quinault
Hoh Rain Forest, in the Hoh Rain Forest
July Creek, North shore of Lake Quinault
Kalaloch, at Kalaloch
Mora, near La Push
North Fork, E. of Lake Quinault
Queets, 14 miles up the Queets Road from US 101
South Beach, near Kalaloch

Some of these campgrounds may be closed in winter. For more information about road conditions and the Olympic National Park campgrounds contact the Olympic National Park 24 hour message line at 360-565-3130 or call 360-565-3131 or check their web site at http://www.nps.gov/olym.

Campgrounds provided by **Washington State Parks** along the Washington coast are:

Bogachiel State Park, south of Forks
Fort Canby State Park, near Ilwaco
Grayland Beach State Park, Grayland
Ocean City State Park, just north of Ocean Shores
Pacific Beach State Park, Pacific Beach
Twin Harbors State Park, south of Westport

For more information on Washington State Parks and these campgrounds, contact Washington State Parks at 1-800-233-0321 or check their website at www.parks.wa.gov.

Some state parks offer reservations. Call Reservations Northwest at 800-452-5687 for further information.

There are a few coastal **Olympic National Forest campgrounds**. They include:

Campbell Tree Grove (Wynoochee Valley)
Coho (Wynoochee Valley)
Falls Creek (Lake Quinault)
Gatton Creek (Lake Quinault)
Willaby (Lake Quinault)
Wynoochee Falls (Wynoochee Valley)

More information of these campgrounds is available by contacting the Olympic National Forest Service at 360-956-2401 or by checking their web site at www.fs.fed.us/r6/olympic.

The **Department of Natural Resources** has campgrounds with limited facilities available along the coast (no running water, vault toilets). These campgrounds include:

Bear Creek, near Sappho, north of Forks
Cottonwood, Hoh River valley
Hoh Oxbow, Hoh River valley
Willoughby Creek, Hoh River valley
Minnie Petersen, on the way to the Hoh Rain Forest
Copper Mine Bottom, east of Kalaloch
Upper Clearwater, east of Kalaloch
Yahoo Lake, east of Kalaloch

More information of these campgrounds can be obtained by contacting the Forks office of DNR at 800-527-3305 or 360-374-6131.

INDEX

FIELD NOTES

_____

_____

_____

_____

_____

_____

_____

_____

_____

_____

_____

_____